BARRON'S
BUSINESS
LIBRARY

Business Banking

Second Edition

Theodore A. Platz, Jr.
Former Vice Chairman, Key Centurion Bancshares, Inc.
and Thomas P. Fitch

General editor for the first edition of *Banking* in *Barron's Business Library* Series is George T. Friedlob, a professor in the School of Accountancy at Clemson University.

© Copyright 2001 by Barron's Educational Series, Inc.
First edition previously titled *Banking* © copyright 1991 by Theodore A. Platz, Jr.

All inquiries should be addressed to:
Barron's Educational Series, Inc.
250 Wireless Boulevard
Hauppauge, New York 11788
http://www.barronseduc.com

International Standard Book No. 0-7641-1398-4

Library of Congress Catalog Card No. 00-034287

Library of Congress Cataloging-in-Publication Data

Platz, Theodore A.
 Business banking / Theodore A. Platz, Jr.—2nd ed. / revised by Thomas P.
 Fitch.
  p. cm.—(Barron's Business Library)
 Rev. ed. of: Banking. c1991.
 Includes index.
 ISBN 0-7641-1398-4
 1. Banks and banking. 2. Bank loans. 3. Small business—Finance.
I. Fitch, Thomas P. II. Platz, Theodore A. Banking. III. Title. IV. Series.
HG1601 .P63 2001
332.1—dc21

00-034287

PRINTED IN THE UNITED STATES OF AMERICA
9 8 7 6 5 4 3 2 1

Contents

Preface to Second Edition

This book is written for entrepreneurs and small business owners who maintain checking or investment accounts with a commercial bank or thrift institution or who look to their bank as a source of financing. Small businesses represent about 95 percent of the businesses operating in the United States, which have many varied banking needs. Business owners have often turned to community-based financial institutions for the convenience, personal service, and access to financing they offer business customers. Throughout this book we use the term "bank" in discussing services available. What is said about banks can also apply to thrift institutions (savings and loans and savings banks). Thrifts in many states also service business checking accounts and underwrite commercial loans.

The business of banking has gone through many changes, mostly for the better, over the last ten years. The banking industry as a whole is healthier and in better financial condition than during the "credit crunch" of 1990–91, when banks across the United States sharply curtailed their lending activities in the face of an economic recession and a pile of deteriorating loans secured by real estate. Banks learned their lessons from that period, and today they are more inclined to look to a borrower's cash flow from business operations than collateral as the source of loan repayment. The deposit insurance system has been strengthened and the cost of insurance is tied to financial risk; better capitalized banks pay a lower cost of deposit insurance than weak banks. Bank customers now have access to more information about their bank's financial condition, which is accessible on the Internet from banking regulators and other sources, so they can more easily pick the bank best matching their needs.

The first several chapters in this updated edition discuss how to select a bank and evaluate your bank's financial health. Also reviewed are important bank services, such as deposit accounts, cash management, and trust services. The next several chapters (chapters 9 through 18) review the steps in presenting a loan request, from initial contact with your loan account officer to common types of loans, including recent enhancements to the Small Business Administration guaranteed loan program. The final chapter discusses options when it's time to change banks. Included in the appendix of this book are two new directories, an Internet Resource directory and a listing of related books and sources of information for further reading.

Thomas P. Fitch

About This Book

INTRODUCTION AND MAIN POINTS

Chapter 1 provides an overview of how this book can improve your understanding of your bankers' needs and thus help you establish a better working relationship with them.

After reading this chapter:

■ You will understand how this book will help you deal with your banker so that you get the money and the service you're entitled to.

■ You will know the kind of businessperson for whom this book has been designed.

■ You will know how to best use this book with the least investment of your time.

HOW CAN THE BOOK HELP?

This book will show you how to make your banker believe in you and your company and help you get more dollars and better service from your bank on better terms than you've been able to get before. It will give you insight into how a bank operates and how it makes money. For those of you who have to borrow, this book will help you understand just what's going on in your banker's mind whenever you seek to borrow money. Finally, this book will help you to be a more effective advocate for your company and to make your banker more effective on your behalf.

This book is based upon the premise that the better you know and understand your bank and the environment in which it works, the better you're going to fare in your dealings with it. If you've ever taken a course on salesmanship, you know that one of the big secrets in making a sale is simply fulfilling or satisfying the needs of the prospective customer. It's not persuasiveness. It's not debating skills. It's not an ability to beat down resistance or apply lots of pressure. It's simply a matter of discovering the needs of a prospect and demonstrating how your product can help satisfy those needs.

The Banker Is Your Prospect

A bank is looking for a satisfactory level of profits on its operations. It attempts to make a profit by borrowing money from its depositors and investing that money in securities and loans. A bank thus has two different groups of customers: depositors and borrowers. It must keep both in mind whenever it is dealing with either one of them.

Generally speaking, there isn't much flexibility in a bank's posted deposit rates, and most customers must simply accept them. But if you're a large customer—one with total deposits of $100,000 or so—then you may be able to create some flexibility for yourself. Much the same is true of fees and service charges: the greater your deposits, the fewer the fees you have to pay. However, even if you don't have big balances, there are circumstances under which you can get charges lowered or reversed. In either case, keep in mind that, like you, bankers have operating costs and are looking for profits. If you can demonstrate that a relationship with you will be profitable for the bank, you'll have room for negotiating better rates and lower fees.

Loans are a different matter, even though borrowers are also looked at by banks as a potential source of profit. The difficulty is that with loans, what's really at issue is the "probable" profitability, which assumes your full and timely repayment of the loan, not the actual profitability. That's why it's important for you to convince your banker that your loan will be repaid on time. Make no mistake about it. When you go to the bank to request a loan, you're going there to make a sale. You should know ahead of time what kind of information the bank will need and what it will want to know about you, your company, and the type of loan you're seeking. The last half of this book is devoted to showing you how to do that.

Understanding and Evaluating Your Bank

There are plenty of negative banker stereotypes. And, unfortunately, there are some bankers who fit those stereotypes all too well. By and large, though, bankers are pretty much like any other group of people. They exhibit a wide assortment of personalities, talents, and skills.

But if you've assumed that all bankers resemble the stereotypes you see on TV or in the movies, then you may be in for a surprise. Many banks are anxious to win as many new customers and as much new business as possible, including depositors and borrowers, as well as customers for their trust departments and their international and investment banking operations. If the bank you're dealing with now doesn't seem like that kind, if it doesn't seem interested in serving you well and in furthering its relationship with you, then maybe it's time for you to consider another bank. In that case, a quick look at the chapters on changing banks or bankers might help. Those chapters, and others in this book, will help you evaluate your present banker . . . and help you pick out a new one if that's what's appropriate.

The book also discusses how you, as a borrower, should deal with your banker when profits or cash flow are poor. When do you let your bank in on the bad news? How much should you divulge and what's the best way to present it? What can you do to help make sure your bank is there when you need it most?

Other chapters in the book describe the different kinds of notes and rates available. There's a chapter on collateral and the impact it can have on your loan and your company. Another focuses on your company's financial statements—are they doing a good job for you? Can they do a better job?

In short, before you go to your bank with a loan request or a request to change the terms of an existing loan, or before you select a new bank, browse through this book and use the appropriate chapters to help you and your company get the money and services you need.

WHO'S THE BOOK FOR?

If you're a small businessman and your borrowing relationship doesn't seem to be what it ought to be, it's possible that you're a bigger part of the problem than your bank is. You may be so busy with the day-to-day operation of your business that you just don't have time to spend on financial planning or financial statements.

You may be ill prepared or in desperate need when you finally realize that you can no longer postpone a visit to the bank to request a loan. Not only have you made ineffective use of your time and the bank's time, but far more importantly, you may wind up with less money or poorer terms and conditions than you could have had otherwise.

The same goes for depositors. If you've ever shopped around for rates, you know that it takes a lot of time, maybe even more time than it's really worth. This book will help you get better mileage out of your time and your deposits, will show you how to get the bank to give you the best rates it has, and will help you decide how far you want to push your relationship to get those kind of rates.

If you've got a good handle on your time and your business, or if your business is simply not that hectic, this book can still help you. Maybe you're one of those borrowers who doesn't feel comfortable with numbers or bankers or financial jargon. This book will give you insights into financial statements and cash flows that will not only help you deal with your bank more effectively but will help you manage your own finances. Also included are simple and practical guidelines for coming up with the figures that make it easier for your bank to understand your business. That will make your bank more comfortable about lending money to your company.

If you're an accountant, you've probably already developed good relationships with several banks and most of what's said in this book will not be new to you. But giving this book to those of your customers who are borrowers should help them get ready for the next bout with their banker. The book can also help reinforce much of the advice you've no doubt already given your clients.

Even if you're in the banking business, this book may provide you with insight. As you already know, the loan side and the deposit side of banking are very different worlds, and making a career move from one to the other can be quite difficult. This book should answer many of the questions you have if you are considering such a move.

In a bank, there's no single route to the top. Even so, the top decisionmakers of many banks are former loan officers. And those who weren't loan officers probably picked up many of the basics of commercial lending while they were moving up the ladder. So if you're not a loan officer now, this book will help educate you about the loan side of your bank.

If you're not involved with a business or with a banking career but are simply concerned with your own personal loans or deposits, you may find much of the material in this book helpful and interesting. You'll find that most of the rules that apply to business depositors apply to ordinary depositors as well. Much the same goes for personal loans: borrowers have to make banks clearly understand their needs and convince banks of their ability to repay.

Some individuals feel uncomfortable asking a bank for a loan; it's as though they regard a loan request as an admission of financial inadequacy or of their failure to save enough or earn enough. But there's nothing wrong with borrowing when the need arises. In fact, it's a good way to enjoy now rather than later or to capitalize on investments or other opportunities that simply won't be available later. Like so many other things, borrowing can be helpful or harmful. Which one it will be depends largely upon you and your banker.

For the many entrepreneurs, contractors, store owners, moms-and-pops, and others who just haven't got lots of spare time, this book provides quick menus for selecting areas to focus on. You'll find it easy to pick out topics from the table of contents and index that suggest opportunities for change or for adding to your bottom line.

As a borrower, it doesn't matter if you're a wholesaler or a retailer, a manufacturer or a distributor. This book will help you anticipate what your banker will want to know about you and your business. Whether you've venturing into the world of tax shelters, looking for real estate to buy, or thinking of investing in a business venture on the side, anticipating what the banker will want to know could mean the difference between achieving your goal and just another pipe dream.

HOW TO READ THIS BOOK

This book has no beginning or ending as such, no plot, no sequential buildup of information that makes it necessary for you to work your way straight through. To get as much as possible from the book, first look at the index or the table of contents. Find a chapter or section that sounds interesting or applicable to your situation. Read it and then browse through the other parts of the book.

The book contains many headings and subheadings, which make it easier for you to skip around and sample different topics. Satisfy your curiosity, and then ... before you go in to see your banker about a loan, prepare a scenario for your visit based on what you've learned from this book. Then make your appointment and stick to your scenario. You should be smiling all the way back from the bank.

CHAPTER PERSPECTIVE

This is not a book to be consumed in a few sittings. It is a reference text, to be consulted from time to time as needs or concerns arise. Let the index and the table of contents be your guide. Pick out a chapter or section that deals with an area in which you feel you're weak or could use some insight. Then jump around from chapter to chapter; come back to some chapters later on. You'll find you're on your way to a better relationship with your bank than you've ever had before.

How Banks Work

INTRODUCTION AND MAIN POINTS

This chapter provides a brief explanation of what a typical bank does and how it's organized.

After studying the material in this chapter:

■ You'll know how a bank attracts and prices the funds it uses to make loans and investments.

■ You'll know why most banks prefer to make loans instead of simply putting their money into bonds and other safer investments.

■ You'll understand why banks put much of their funds—money not being lent—in a variety of bonds and other lower-yielding financial instruments.

■ You'll know why banks offer other financial services to their customers.

PROFITS AND SPREADS

Commercial banks, like many other companies, are in business to make money for their shareholders. They do this by borrowing money at interest rates that are lower than the rates they earn on the loans and investments they make with that money. The spread between these two types of rates has to be large enough to cover the operating costs banks incur. Hence, a bank's principal activities revolve around gathering deposits and placing this money in either loans or investments of various kinds. Virtually everything else a bank does is intended to make it more attractive to depositors and borrowers.

A Sample Income-and-Expense Statement

In order for a bank to be profitable, its operating costs must be recouped from its "spread"—the difference between what the bank pays for its deposits and what it earns on its loans and investments. A rough rule of thumb is that for every dollar of noninterest expense (salaries and cost of buildings and computers, for example) a bank incurs, it has to earn a little more than two dollars. And that's after taking into account the income from fees, service charges, and other non-loan services connected with deposit accounts.

The bank also has to set aside about 50 cents for potential losses it suffers on the loans it makes (the reserve for loan losses). Finally, a bank has to pay half a dollar or so in state and federal income taxes, which leaves it with about one dollar of profit. It pays approximately a third of that to its shareholders and retains the other two-thirds for contingencies and future growth. That one dollar of profit works out to be a return on equity of around 15 percent and a return on total assets (a misleading but nevertheless popular industry measure) of something over 1 percent.

Suppose a bank has total assets of $100 and capital of $7. Figure 2-1 shows how its profit-and-loss statement might look.

FIGURE 2-1 *Hypothetical profit-and-loss statement*

Interest income		$10.00
Interest expense		–6.25
Net interest income		$3.75
Provision for loan losses		– .50
		$3.25
Non-interest income	+1.50	
Non-interest expense	–3.25	
Net income before taxes		$1.50
Taxes		–.50
Net income after taxes		$1.00
Dividends to shareholders		.33
Retained for growth, to meet regulators' capital requirements, and for contingencies		.67
		$1.00

It should be emphasized that these figures are very rough. The way profits are produced varies enormously from bank to bank. Banks range in size from very tiny institutions with only $5 to $10 million of assets to money-market giants with hundreds of billions of dollars of assets. The interest they earn and pay out is a blend not only of the high-rate and low-rate products for which they have been able to develop current markets but also of rates left over from rate structures that prevailed in earlier years. For instance, a bank's pay-out includes certificates of deposit bought not only at current interest rates but also at other rates, higher or lower, that were in effect months or years earlier.

Banks also vary in function. Some are essentially deposit gatherers that make few or no loans. These may be small, single-unit banks in outlying areas or much bigger banks with extensive branch networks but relatively little opportunity to put money to work in their own territory. Other banks are very heavily oriented toward commercial loans. They make loans that in the aggregate exceed their total deposits by a considerable margin, and are therefore forced to depend on a variety of sources—not just deposits—for their funding. This makes for a much more complex organizational structure and range of operation.

Banks are in the difficult position of serving masters with different goals: depositors and borrowers. Depositors, of course, want to receive the highest interest rates for their money; borrowers naturally seek to pay the lowest rates possible. In addition, banks are service organizations whose costs of operation are not always readily apparent, which makes customers more sensitive to charges and fees than they might be otherwise. This sensitivity has been heightened because banks are increasingly charging for services, such as checking accounts, that they once provided for free, choosing to compete on interest rates instead of on the range of services they offer. In addition to regular checking accounts, which do not pay interest, banks have Negotiable Order of Withdrawal (NOW) accounts, which are deposit accounts with check-writing privileges. NOW accounts can be opened by consumers and certain types of businesses (such as nonprofit organizations and sole proprietorship business owners).

THE DEPOSIT SIDE OF THE BANK

The banking industry handles millions of deposit transactions every day, ranging from multimillion-dollar transfers to those involving less than a dollar. Some transactions pass through the hands of tellers; others are automated, like the computer-to-computer deposits of payroll or Social Security payments to personal accounts. All of these transactions are nothing more than transfers of money from one account to another.

In recent years, there has been an explosion in the variety of deposit accounts available to customers. In addition to the traditional savings and non-interest-bearing checking accounts, banks now offer a variety of interest-bearing checking accounts, certificates of deposit, IRAs, repurchase agreements, sweep accounts, statement savings accounts—all with rules, rates, and maturities that differ from one bank to the next. To make matters more confusing, these similar deposit vehicles are called by different names from bank to bank. Consequently, bank customers find it difficult to make comparisons; instead, they must study features thoroughly and make selections based upon their particular needs.

Deposit Pricing

The interest rate paid on a bank's deposits follows closely the rate of return the bank can generate through investment, and the rate offered the largest depositors may be very close to the bank's own rate of return. Not surprisingly, the bigger a deposit account is, the more vigorously it is pursued by banks; deposits from corporations with excess funds are aggressively solicited, as are those from state and municipal agencies. Typically, these deposits, generally $1 million or more, are used by the bank to finance its own investments of an equal amount at a rate that is just a little bit higher than the rates it must pay to the company, state, or municipality. Thus, the rate paid to the depositor depends largely upon the investment rates that are available to the bank at the time. Because the competition for this kind of deposit business is so keen, spreads may be as little as a sixteenth or an eighth of a percent. Even so, small spreads add up quickly. Furthermore, this banking activity can be handled by a small staff; one person can easily generate many times his or her salary in the profit these transactions produce.

Rates on smaller deposits are determined by a variety of factors, such as the size of the bank and the community it serves. In many small banks, the president is the primary or sole rate setter, using a variety of sources of published rates, including newspapers and rate sheets from bigger banks in nearby cities. Rates at most banks are set by what are known as asset and liability committees (ALCOs), which evaluate rates and other information on loan demand and deposit supply gathered from the banks in the community.

Although antitrust laws prohibit banks from jointly agreeing on the interest rates to be set, many banks do call their competitors in the guise of customers to find out what's being offered. Some banks adjust, or at least review, their rates daily. Others do it weekly or even less frequently, waiting until customer complaints, major rate shifts, or some other occurrence dictates a change.

A bank wants to pay no more than necessary to gather deposits sufficient to achieve its financial goals. Consequently, a bank with a heavy loan demand is likely to pay better rates than a nearby bank with little or no demand for loans. Many banks, in fact, peg their interest rates directly to the demand for loans, in order to assure themselves of the funds they need. Nearly all banks have some customers who are "rate sensitive" and move their money around from one bank to another as rate opportunities suggest. But most customers are not like that. For example, many leave their money in low-rate savings accounts or in non-interest-bearing checking accounts when they could be earning much more on this money invested in, say, a certificate of deposit.

Check Clearing

A very important part of any bank's activities is the conversion of checks into interest-earning assets. That happens when checks are physically delivered to the banks on which they are drawn and funds are transferred to the banks of deposit. Thanks to computers, the magnetic ink now used to encode checks, and a highly efficient system of check transfer, more than 90 percent of all check deposits can be drawn on just one business day later.

To convert checks into earning assets as quickly as possible, banks have local arrangements (known as check clearing houses) under which they exchange each other's checks one or more times each day, debiting or crediting accounts they maintain with each other for the value of checks exchanged. Similar arrangements with large out-of-town banks, called *correspondent banks* because they process checks for many smaller banks, and with the Federal Reserve Banks, make it possible to convert into cash checks drawn on any bank in the country in a matter of days. The Federal Reserve System's own network of check collection centers, the Regional Check Processing Centers, and the 12 district Federal Reserve banks function as the backbone of the U.S. interbank check processing system, supplementing local check clearing houses and correspondent bank networks to help maintain an efficient nationwide payment system.

A process called check truncation promises to simplify matters even further by temporarily storing, then destroying, all checks at the bank of initial deposit. Instead of forwarding the cancelled checks to the customer's bank (for return to the customer along with the monthly checking account statement), the depositing bank would make copies of checks processed on a computer readable CD-ROM for retrieval if necessary at a later date. While check truncation has not caught on for a variety of reasons, many banks offer business customers a service called *check safekeeping*. In check safekeeping, the customer's bank keeps the cancelled checks, and on request will forward copies of individual checks or a CD-ROM readable file listing all checks paid. Businesses that issue a large number of checks like the convenience of getting check copies on a CD-ROM because the computer readable format makes it much easier to look up individual checks and compare the bank statement against their accounting record of checks issued for any accounting period.

THE LOAN SIDE
Consumer Loans

The loan side of banking can be divided into two broad categories: consumer loans and commercial loans. Consumer loans are those that are repaid through monthly installments. At some banks, the term also encompasses demand loans and loans that mature every 90 days or so. Consumer loans are either secured (that is, backed by collateral) or unsecured, and are used mainly for financing major purchases and consolidating debt. Most consumer loans mature anywhere from six months to five or ten years from the time they are granted.

Mortgage Loans

Mortgage loans, like consumer loans, lend themselves to formularization, and bank personnel who evaluate mortgage applications follow certain mathematical rules of thumb that don't vary too much from one bank to another. Commercial banks and thrifts (savings banks and savings-and-loan associations) offer fixed-rate mortgages, variable-rate mortgages, and, frequently, both. As a rule, mortgage loans are not kept by the bank but are sold off to long-term investors such as insurance companies and pension and profit-sharing plans.

Commercial Loans

Commercial loans are entirely different from consumer loans. Every commercial loan represents a unique situation, one that cannot be analyzed using simple formulas like those associated with consumer loans. There *are* broad rules used in the analysis of commercial credits, but they are normally viewed against the history and prospects of the company requesting the loan. Not surprisingly, this kind of analysis can be performed only by personnel with special training and skills. In many smaller banks, the president is the only one who handles such loans. Most larger banks employ officers specially trained to handle commercial loans. These officers usually handle most of the borrower's other banking business as well.

Commercial loan departments of many larger banks are divided into groups that specialize in companies of a certain size, industry, or geographical location. They may even have high net worth groups that minister to the financial needs of only the wealthiest of the bank's customers.

Interest rates on commercial loans can be fixed or floating, and the life of the loans can vary from one day to five or ten years. Because interest rates have fluctuated considerably since World War II, most commercial banks today are not interested in fixing rates for more than three to five years; most prefer to use a rate that is pegged to the prime rate, a nationwide rate banks charge their better customers. Whether the rate is fixed or floating and whether it's at prime or above prime are matters that are negotiated separately for each loan. Loan rates are usually set, within well-established guidelines, by individual loan officers. Frequently, a loan officer's rate is changed during the approval process.

OTHER BANKING SERVICES
Investments

Banks would prefer to put all of their money into loans if they could, because most loans produce a higher rate of return, even after allowing for losses on loans that go sour, than any other option. The problem is that there just isn't enough demand for loans to use up the cumulative capital of all the banks in business; in addition, loan demand fluctuates with seasons and business cycles. The bank has yet another group of people, usually called the Investment Department, that spends its time putting the rest of the bank's money to work at the best rates it can find. That job is complicated by the fact that the amount of money available for investment in bonds and other nonloan financial vehicles fluctuates seasonally, monthly, weekly, daily, and even by the hour because of changes in loan demand and deposit levels as bank customers move their money. To deal with this, the bank keeps part of its investment portfolio highly liquid, ready to be sold off the moment the need arises.

But there's a price to liquidity. As a rule, the greater an investment's liquidity, the lower the interest it returns. So banks usually keep in their portfolios a few highly liquid investments, supplemented by less liquid, but higher-yielding, securities. Federal deposit insurance has virtually eliminated a major need for liquidity: the need to provide funds in the event of a run on the bank. Consequently, the primary purpose of investment portfolios has become putting to work excess funds—namely, the money that a bank has not been able to float in the form of higher-yielding loans.

Rate levels move up and down not only because of changes in current basic economic conditions but because of changes in people's expectations about future conditions. The changes in rates alter the prices of stocks (which banks do not invest in for their own account), bonds, and any other instrument whose rate of interest is fixed. (For instance, if interest rates decline, the market value of existing bonds will rise.) Some banks buy U.S. Treasury bills (T-bills) or government bonds and simply hold them until they mature; others trade in and out of them as opportunities arise. There is a wide variety of instruments banks use to sop up excess funds, including fed funds (so called because they used to represent money left over in accounts at the Federal Reserve Bank), repurchase agreements (repos), reverse repos, T-bills (which mature in less than one year), and government notes (which mature in two to 10 years) and bonds (which mature in more than 10 years). A repo is the purchase of a security with the understanding that the seller will buy it back by some agreed-upon date, usually one day later.

The complexity and unpredictability of investing leftover bank funds makes it a challenging job. It is an important banking activity, a bank's alternative to making loans.

Loan losses by commercial banks average three-tenths to five-tenths of one percent, including credit card losses. If you consider loan losses as a cost of doing business and then take that cost away from the interest rates earned on loans, you can see that the net yield is still much better than that on Treasury bills, government notes and bonds, and on other investments available to banks. A quick look at rates in *The Wall Street Journal* will confirm that for you.

The Trust Department

Many larger banks have trust departments and regard them as yet another service that helps attract deposit and loan customers. Some of these departments are profitable; many are not. The trust department is a department with which you should become familiar. It won't add a thing to your current profitability, but it can make a tremendous difference to your family if you should die. Despite the fact that the bank, like your accountant and your lawyer, can make money by planning your estate and handling it when you die or become incapacitated, you should hear what they have to say then act accordingly.

Trust departments can also help you in other ways. For example, they can help you take care of profit-sharing and pension plans, ESOPS (employee stock ownership plans), Keogh and H.R. 10 plans (pension plans for the self-employed), and investment matters you may be too busy to properly care for.

The International Department

International departments of banks provide services such as letters of credit (either import or export), handle inquiries about conditions or companies in foreign countries, and offer advice about foreign currencies and exchange risks. Generally speaking, only large, metropolitan-area banks have international departments, though some of the functions of an international department are found at smaller banks, where they are handled by commercial loan officers. If a small bank doesn't have a certain service itself, it normally will work with larger correspondents in nearby cities to get the services its customers need.

Many large banks have not only sizable international operations here in this country but extensive branch and correspondent bank networks abroad. Through those networks, they can provide a domestic company operating abroad with virtually all the bank services available in this country or help it locate such services. Here again, though, the purpose is to provide customers with the services they need so that they will keep their loan and deposit business with the bank.

Other Services

There are a variety of other services offered by banks, such as safe-deposit boxes, buying and selling of bonds, and discount brokerage services. Other banking services include check cashing, handling credit inquiries, and offering drive-in facilities, night-deposit drops, payroll services, and equipment leasing.

REGULATION

Because of the importance of money to our economy, banks are subject to a considerable and growing amount of regulation. This regulation is designed to promote the well-being of the banking system and the overall economic health of the country. It is aimed at avoiding the financial panics that periodically racked the nation during the 1800s and the early 1900s. The Federal Reserve System, founded in 1913 to deal with such panics and otherwise guide the economy, functions today as one of the industry's principal regulators. It also serves the national economy by providing a money-transfer system for the banking industry.

Equally important to the nation's overall economic health is the safety of depositors' money. The stock-market crash of 1929 and the widespread bank problems that followed resulted in the creation of the Federal Deposit Insurance Corporation, under which the federal government provides insurance that guarantees virtually all depositors that the money they put in a bank up to specified limits will always be immediately available to them.

A third layer of regulation is concerned with the rights of particular groups of consumers. It has grown to the point that its paperwork alone, especially in the area of consumer lending, is believed to add something more than half a percent to the cost of making a loan.

Modernization of the financial services industry added another layer of regulation—*functional regulation* of banks, securities firms, and insurance companies. The Gramm-Leach-Bliley Act of 1999, the landmark legislation lifting most of the Depression-era barriers to cross-industry affiliations, allows banks to underwrite securities and sell insurance and mutual funds, subject to regulatory approval. Commercial banks engaging in mutual fund marketing, for instance, would become subject to the regulatory oversight of the Securities and Exchange Commission, in addition to supervision by their primary banking regulator, the Comptroller of the Currency or, for state-chartered banks, state banking departments.

In banking, regulatory improvements allowing banks to service more of their customers' needs often add new layers of complexity. Nevertheless, the financial industry overhaul set in motion by the Gramm-Leach-Bliley Act reconciles financial industry regulation with events occurring in the marketplace while preserving much of the existing regulatory system.

CHAPTER PERSPECTIVE

Shakespeare's advice was "Never a borrower or a lender be." Banks do both, all the time and at the same time. They are faced with the challenge of balancing conflicting needs of borrowers and depositors, while generating as much fee income as they can. Like any other business, banks have operating costs. They cover some of those costs directly by charging fees for services rendered. They cover the rest indirectly by establishing a sufficiently large spread between interest rates for loans and those for deposits. With what's left over, they absorb losses on loans they've made, pay dividends to their shareholders, and set aside money for contingencies and for growth.

Choosing the Right Bank

INTRODUCTION AND MAIN POINTS

If you're just starting a business, one of the decisions you have to make is where to do your banking. Before you decide that, however, you should ask yourself whether or not you're ever going to borrow from that bank. If the answer is no, then your decision is relatively simple. If you don't know, then you'd be well advised to assume that borrowing will indeed be a part of your future and select a bank accordingly. This chapter begins with a discussion of what a nonborrower should look for when choosing a bank. The rest of the chapter is devoted to selecting a bank with a view toward borrowing from this bank at some point in the future.

After studying the material in this chapter:

■ You'll know how to gather information about banks and how to evaluate their reputations.

■ You'll know how to determine how the backgrounds and skills of members of a bank's board of directors might affect your own banking relationship.

■ You'll know how to estimate a bank's appetite for making loans.

■ You'll know when to use a local bank—and when to use an out-of-town bank—for your borrowing needs.

HOW TO SELECT A BANK

There are many reasons to consider using a bank for your financial needs. If your business needs financing, banks loans are competitive in cost with financing from other sources. A bank loan often has a lower interest rate than loans from nonbank commercial lenders. Some government-backed loan programs may offer loans at below-market interest rates, but low-interest government guaranteed loans are usually available only to qualifying borrowers. Bankers are in contact every day with businesses in many industries, including yours.

Bankers keep up with industry trends and they can offer expert guidance on managing your business or obtaining financing, often at no cost to you. It's part of the banker's job. Borrowing from a bank and repaying the loan on time adds to your credit references and improves your credit rating, or if you're a first-time borrower it can help you get a credit rating. Finally, banks have many other services that can help you run your business more efficiently and service customers at home or around the world. Many banks offer their customers "one-stop shopping" for most, if not all, of their financial needs. If you can understand how banks function and how decisions about loan approvals are made, you will be successful in working with your banker more often than not, as long as you can work within their lending guidelines.

CRITERIA FOR A NONBORROWER

If borrowing is not a major concern of yours, your selection of a bank should be governed by factors such as convenience, charges and fees, earnings credits on balances, rates paid on interest-bearing accounts, branch and automated teller machine (ATM) networks, and availability of any other banking services.

You may be surprised at the wide variety of services banks offer to prospects and customers. Obviously, your company won't need them all. And no single bank is likely to offer all of them.

Convenience

Convenience is probably the most important factor in the selection of a bank. It involves not only the location of the bank and its branches but also its regular and drive-in hours, the locations of its ATMs and ATMs of banks on the same network, and night-deposit facilities. Will you be making daily trips to the bank, or will once a week be enough? How much of your banking business can you do by mail or telephone? Your time is probably limited, and anything that saves you time is going to help you do a better job running your business.

Cost of Services

The next most important factor in choosing a bank is the cost of doing business with the bank—the fees and service charges you incur in the course of your banking activity. As you know from your own business, virtually everything you do for your customers adds to your cost of operation. The same goes for banks. A bank has to cover its expenses with revenues from two sources: charges for services and interest earned on customers' deposits.

Bank fees are charged directly to your account or indirectly to your account analysis (see Chapter 5). Sometimes the charges may seem, and in fact may be, inordinately high. Sometimes that's more a matter of perception than reality, since the costs of performing services are not always readily apparent to customers. In other cases, however, the charge can be a "guesstimated" cost figure, the result of converting known overall costs into thin slices (by dividing the cost figure by the total number of deposits, checks processed, type of accounts, etc.) in order to come up with a specific figure that can be applied to a specific activity. In other instances, charges may be set high in order to discourage certain kinds of activities, such as overdrawing accounts.

The aggressiveness of charges varies from bank to bank. Some banks never let a transaction slip by without assessing a charge. Other banks levy very few charges. Still others use "free" accounts and low service charges to attract new customers, then make up for that lost fee income somewhere else. In any case, charges ultimately come out of your pocket, so you should pay close attention to them.

Ask all banks you are considering for schedules of their charges. Examine these schedules closely and be sure they cover all the things for which your normal account activity is likely to generate charges. Then compare these schedules and determine which bank is most economical for you.

Be sure you also ask for a list of those charges that go into your account analysis. This is particularly important if you have very large and active accounts. Examples of such chargeable activities are deposits, check writing, stop payments, returned checks, wire transfers, account statements, and requests for currency and coins. You should compare the account activity you anticipate with that list and with the bank's published list of charges.

Quality

Like most companies, banks talk a lot about the quality they deliver. To evaluate such claims, it's a good idea to ask your friends and acquaintances, both business and personal, about the quality of service they get at their banks. If one bank keeps popping up as troublesome, difficult to deal with, or inept, chances are you would have the same kind of problems with that bank. Weigh what you hear about quality against price and convenience. This may take some time and effort, but it's easier to select the right bank in the first place than it is to change banks later on.

CRITERIA FOR BORROWERS

All banks have reputations, especially when it comes to their lending activities. The community of borrowers within which any bank operates has a pretty clear idea as to how aggressive or nonaggressive the bank is when it comes to making loans. That reputation may apply to just a branch or a group of branches instead of the entire bank. Listen to the talk at the country club, at business gatherings, at chamber of commerce get-togethers—anyplace where you can find businesspeople who borrow money from banks. Ask those people what their experience has been and what they've heard from friends and business associates. Such conversations usually get around to the individual bank involved.

Complimentary talk about a bank can usually be accepted at face value—with one important caveat. Sometimes the treatment a customer gets is more a sign of that customer's own financial standing than of the understanding and insight of the bank.

The same goes for criticism. It is difficult to evaluate if you don't know something about the financial health of the borrower making the observations. There are few things more wounding to personal or corporate pride than being turned down for a loan. Hence, complaints may be well founded, or they may be the mark of someone who doesn't understand his or her own financial circumstances and who therefore has unreasonable expectations. That's why it's a good idea to get readings from a number of people. Obviously, the more consistent the comments you get about a bank, the more likely they are to be accurate.

A very useful source of information about banks actively lending to small business borrowers is the Small Business Administration's Office of Advocacy. Every year the SBA Office of Advocacy issues a report listing the top "small-business friendly" banks in each state, based on small business lending activity (loans under $1 million) disclosed in bank call reports. In 1991, Congress mandated that financial institutions begin reporting loans to small businesses in their quarterly call reports and this information first became available in 1994.

The SBA report rates bank lenders according to four criteria: 1) the ratio of small business loans to total assets; 2) the ratio of small business loans to total business loans; 3) the dollar value of small business loans; 4) the number of small business loans. The SBA Office of Advocacy's report on lending to small businesses is available on the Internet at *www.sba.gov/advo/stats/lending*.

The SBA lending survey also reports on loans to local communities, which banks are encouraged to make under the Community Reinvestment Act enacted in 1977. However, only banks with assets over $250 million or banks owned by a holding company with assets of $1 billion or more are legally required to disclose their CRA-related lending. Given the accelerating pace of interstate mergers in banking, CRA data will become more important in understanding small business lending by banks in any one state. Banks above $250 million in assets represent only about 18 percent of the banks operating in the United States, but according to the SBA these larger banks make two-thirds of the loans to small businesses.

Personal Loans

Don't use comments about a bank's reputation for making personal loans as a guide to what's in store for your request for a commercial loan. Personal loans—car loans, mortgage loans, and most other installment-type loans—are usually handled on a formula basis. This means that a loan request either meets a few ratio tests or it doesn't. Commercial loans are far more varied and complex, and they call for an entirely different kind of review process.

The Board of Directors

Knowing the makeup of the bank's board of directors is very important, especially in smaller communities. An obvious reason is to be sure that none of your business competitors is on the board. Some banks have procedures for insulating competitors, but these banks are the exception. In small banks, the directors are likely to be actively involved in the loan-approval process. That makes it even more important for you to think about who the directors are. Is the board composed of community blue-bloods or of self-made people? How many of these manage their own companies? Are there a lot of directors whose time is largely spent tending to family holdings created by other generations? How many of the directors are involved with nothing but the bank board?

As a rule, the more directors on the board who are responsible for their own successes, the more likely that bank is to be responsive to your needs. Intentionally or not, the board sets the loan climate within the bank. And the officers you deal with reflect that climate.

You may meet and perhaps get to know a number of the directors. In a sense, they represent a network of connections that might help you at some point down the road. As you no doubt have already discovered, building your own networks can be very important, and the directors of your bank have the potential for being helpful to you when the need arises.

Check out whether the members of the board are actively involved in the various charities around town. It's a good sign if they are, for it suggests that they're in touch with the needs of customers as well. If you want realistic and involved directors, look for those who are already demonstrating those qualities.

Occasionally you may encounter a board member who tries to use the bank position to drum up personal business. It may be an insurance agent who regularly calls on loan applicants and tries to sell them loan insurance to protect the new loans or additional insurance to cover outstanding ones. Or it could be a lawyer, a car dealer, even one of your customers or suppliers. You never know how helpful or harmful a director like that can be to the financing you need.

A board that has members with tarnished reputations is one you should be wary of. Some of the lending activities could be self-dealing, a practice that has led to many bank failures, especially in the savings-and-loan industry. You don't want to hook up with a bank that's on the road to failure.

Banks feel an obligation to do as much as they can, through loans, to help businesses in their community grow and prosper, even though this kind of lending is expensive, time-consuming, and risky. Any bank that limits its lending activities to those with pristine credits ought to reexamine its community philosophy.

As a rule, bank directors are a good and responsible group. Most of them are genuinely interested in the welfare and growth of their bank and are therefore eager to bring in all the new business they can. Still, some boards are much better than others, and some are much more effective at providing the direction and support that is essential for their bank to perform properly. You'll find, when you start asking around, that you can obtain a wealth of information on the quality of any bank's board of directors.

The Loan-to-Deposit Ratio

If you've asked around about a bank's reputation and if you've found out what kind of board members it has, you probably have also learned something about the bank's appetite for loans. Still, it doesn't hurt to double-check your research with a quick financial test—the bank's loan-to-deposit ratio. Ask your account officer about your bank's loan-to-deposit ratio. Or you can calculate it yourself using deposit and loan data from the bank's most recent annual report.

The loan-to-deposit ratio is by far the most reliable measure of a bank's lending activity. It is the dollar amount of its loans calculated as a percent of the total dollars on deposit. Actually, it's more an indicator of the overall economic climate in which a bank is operating than it is a measure of that bank's lending activity. Banks in the same geographical area tend to have similar loan-to-deposit ratios. Differences in ratios from one bank to another are far more meaningful indicators of loan activity than the ratios themselves.

A loan-to-deposit ratio of 70 percent is regarded by many banks as optimal. For your purposes, however, anything over 50 percent or so suggests that the bank wants to make loans and that your loan request will get a decent hearing.

When a bank's loan-to-deposit ratio is low—say, below 40 percent—it may mean that the bank isn't receiving many applications for loans. The significance to you, a would-be borrower, is that the bank is not likely to have many commercial loan officers. This may mean that the bank is likely to take a pretty cautious approach to its lending activities. This is particularly true of smaller banks.

A bank in this situation tends to fall back on more basic lending practices—that is, it lends to people with whom it has already done business. So if you're an unknown quantity, or if you haven't done much borrowing in the past, your chances of getting a sizable loan from this bank are not good. It also doesn't help if the nature of your business is out of the ordinary. You may be permitted to borrow only against what you have—namely, collateral, or your corporate or personal net worth.

You can refine your estimate of a bank's commercial loan activity with a breakdown of the bank's loan figures—that is, a statement showing how much of its total loan figure is made up of commercial loans. The bigger the commercial loan total, the bigger the commercial loan staff and the more likely it is that there will be a loan officer who is sympathetic to your needs. Some banks provide this information on their statements; others don't.

How Far Should You Go to Find the Right Bank?

Simply put, as far as you have to. Normally, the nearest big city is fine. Large companies often use banks scattered all around the country, and the locations of those banks aren't necessarily related in any way to where the companies conduct their business. One caveat, though: Almost all banks prefer to have a local bank involved in loan relationships. That means that if you try to do your borrowing anywhere other than in or near your own town, you should be prepared to explain why you're not dealing with a local bank.

Out-of-town bankers rely on local bankers to provide any news that could have a bearing on the wellbeing of a borrower. Of interest are issues like plant expansions, new product lines, labor and management trouble and growth in the trade.

Asking for a Referral

If your local bank won't give you a loan, ask it to suggest banks that may. And while you're at it, ask your local banker for an introduction. Most bankers will be delighted at the opportunity to soften the impact of their decline in this way.

Bankers know there's a chance that your company may make it big someday. If they can't meet your financing needs, they'll usually be happy to hang on to some of your deposit business while another bank takes care of the loans. Banking history is full of stories about loan turndowns that bankers wish they'd never made. It's also full of stories about borrower loyalty to a bank because that bank made a loan that was probably more an act of faith than a rational credit decision. While the new bank will get the loans and most of the deposit accounts, see if you can keep something at the local bank, like payroll accounts or personal checking accounts. They're an effective way of keeping in touch locally, a way of keeping the door open and the contact going.

CHAPTER PERSPECTIVE

It's important to select the right bank. If you're going to be just a depositor at that bank, you can focus on convenience, price, and quality of service. It's important that your banking be fairly routine and not consume a lot of your time.

If you're going to be a borrower, it's even more important that you select the right bank. You need a bank that will give you all that you're entitled to, that you can count on when the going gets tough, and that responds quickly and fairly. Talk to members of the borrowing community. They'll be able to give you a good idea of the lending personalities of nearby banks. This will help you select the right bank the first time.

Evaluating Your Bank's Health

INTRODUCTION AND MAIN POINTS

This chapter discusses the potential impact on you of the failure or near failure of your bank.

After studying the material in this chapter:

▬ You'll know the likely impact on you if you are a depositor at a bank that fails.

▬ You'll know the possible impact on you if you are a borrower at a bank that fails or nearly fails.

▬ You'll know how to calculate and evaluate some simple ratios for determining how well or poorly your bank is doing.

▬ You'll know how to evaluate the quality of your bank's earnings.

DEPOSITOR INSURANCE

Federal deposit insurance protects most depositors, whether their accounts are in commercial banks, thrifts, or credit unions. Generally, the limit of the insurance is $100,000 for all funds owned in the same right and capacity within the same bank. This is true whether the money is in one account or scattered over many, whether in one branch or several. Banks obtain deposit insurance from a number of sources: the Bank Insurance Fund (BIF), the Savings Association Insurance Fund (SAIF), and NCUA (National Credit Union Administration). The Bank Insurance Fund, insuring deposits in commercial banks, and the Savings Association Insurance Fund, insuring thrift institution deposits, are managed by the FDIC. Most banks provide booklets that explain in considerable detail how the insurance works. The booklets tell you which accounts are covered and which are not. There is insurance for corporation and partnership accounts, in addition to personal accounts. There is also coverage for IRA, Keogh, pension, and profit-sharing plans.

There are two other things about which you ought to be concerned if you're a depositor at a bank that fails. First, there could be a few days' delay before you get paid for what you had in the bank. The second concern arises if you have more than $100,000 in the bank and interest has accumulated, in which case you are uninsured for the amount by which your account exceeds $100,000. If your bank becomes insolvent, the FDIC is under no obligation to pay 100 percent of your deposit claim; uninsured depositors are at risk to the extent their deposits exceed $100,000 per account. If you have any doubts concerning your coverage after you've studied the matter fully, you may want to spread your accounts over two or more banks. This move has a price—the reduction of your clout as a big depositor at any one bank.

Very few banks are actually liquidated by the insurer. They are usually auctioned off, in whole or in part, as discussed below, to one or more banks, which assume all deposit obligations. Of course, there is a risk to depositors here: the new bank has the right to reduce interest rates. That includes a certificate of deposit that still has months or years to go before it matures.

THE IMPACT OF BANK FAILURE ON BORROWERS
Auctioning Off a Failed Bank

When regulators deem a bank to be a failure, they shut it down. The FDIC steps in and arranges an orderly transfer, through an auction process, of the failed bank's assets and deposit liabilities to another bank. The winning bidder reopens the bank—often within just a few hours of its having been shut down. The bank's customers may not even be aware of the change in management until sometime later. When a buyer cannot be found, the failed bank is liquidated, its depositors are paid from the Bank Insurance Fund, the commercial bank deposit insurance fund, and the FDIC attempts to sell the bank's assets (mostly loans with principal and interest payments paid to date, or "good" loans) to other financial institutions.

The bank that wins the auction not only pays a premium to the FDIC but also supplies the capital necessary to support the deposit liabilities it has just acquired. This bank also gets the good loans and investments of the failed bank, and receives cash from the insurer to make up the difference so that its newly acquired assets, including the cash minus the premium, equals the sum of the assumed deposits. It is a simple process, but it isn't wrinkle-free. One of the wrinkles is that borrowers, as a result of the sale of their loans, undergo a change in their borrowing relationships.

The Bad-Loan Pool

But there's a bigger wrinkle: you may wind up in the insurance agency's bad-loan pool. When that happens, you are forced to deal with "lenders" (the FDIC) who really don't want your business.

You wind up in the bad-loan pool either because you come upon hard times and are not healthy financially or because you negotiated some rates in the past that are below the current prevailing market levels. Either of those two conditions makes your loan unattractive to the successor bank, with the result that it won't buy your loan in the initial takeover transaction.

Sometimes, insurers are able to package the low-interest loans they've acquired and sell them off at a discount.

You may be left with one bank for your deposit accounts and one or more banks for your different loans. If that sounds strange, it's really not. Of course, if you're a poor credit risk, your loan isn't likely to be sold anyway, and you'll wind up with the insurer. This means that the next time you want to rearrange your loan or do anything other than simply make payments (release or substitute collateral, for example), the answer you're likely to get is "no." If you need to borrow new money, even for a short period of time, or borrow under a line of credit arranged previously, you're probably going to have to find a new bank. And that could be very difficult if your business has come upon hard times, if money is tight, or if new, higher interest rates put a dent in your cash flow.

A Failing Bank Means Changes Are Likely

Sooner or later, a bank in poor health undergoes changes in management, and that can mean changes in your relationship with the bank. The change in management can come about either as a result of forces from within, after top management decides new policies or officers are in order, or through a sale of the bank. The latter can be the result of a takeover arranged by the board as a way of bringing in better management, or it can come through a hostile takeover.

A survey of corporate customers of banks indicated that, of those whose banks had been taken over by another bank or bank holding company, one-third experienced a change in their relationship. Of those, about half thought the relationship had improved and half thought it had deteriorated. Remember that the survey included *all* banks taken over, for whatever reason. Had the survey been confined to takeovers of problem banks headed toward failure, the number of firms reporting a deterioration in their relationship would no doubt have been much higher. However they come about, changes in management likely mean changes in loan policies, and that kind of change can have an effect on your borrowing arrangements.

SOME SIMPLE RATIOS FOR EVALUATING A BANK

Steering clear of a failing bank could be one of the most important decisions you make. If you take the time to calculate the following ratios, you can quickly get a feel for the health of the bank you're considering. The ratios are easy to calculate, and the only data you'll need are a few numbers you can easily find in the bank's annual report.

Return on Assets

The return on assets ratio (ROA) is often included in the brief summary that many banks provide in the first page or two of their annual reports. It's the bank's net income for the year calculated as a percent of its total assets—or average total assets for the year. An ROA over 1 percent is generally considered good; anything less than that needs improving. So think hard before you do business with a bank earning less than one half of one percent on its assets, especially if that's been the case for a couple of years.

You should also check out a bank closely even if it's earning too much money—say, over 2 percent or so on assets. The high earnings may be the result of the bank's doing a good job keeping costs in line; on the other hand, high earnings may be the result of high loan rates. Ask around and see if that's the case.

A high ROA can also be the result of an accumulation of excess capital through some combination of good earnings and low dividends. What constitutes excess capital? It depends. Banking regulators are now imposing new, stiffer requirements that base the levels of required capital upon the degree of risk inherent in the assets the bank holds. Some large regional and money-center banks have struggled to bring their capital up from levels of 4 or 5 percent to the 8 percent average capital-to-assets ratio required by banking regulations, while many small banks are comfortably capitalized at the 7-to-10-percent range.

Anything over that is a plus for you in two ways: one, it's an extra measure of safety for your deposits in the event that the bank comes upon hard times; and, two, the extra capital is the equivalent of a pool of free or low-cost money available for the bank to invest. That's because dividends paid to shareholders are usually considerably less than the interest the bank would have to pay to depositors for a similar amount of funds.

ROA is far and away the most widely used measure of performance in the banking industry. A healthy ROA means that there's little likelihood of any major changes in a bank's management or loan policies. That in turn means there's little likelihood that you'll have to go through changes later that could be unsettling to your lending arrangements. A good ROA could also mean that there's less pressure on management for high loan rates, low deposit rates, and cutbacks in services.

Return on Equity

Return on equity (ROE), like ROA, is often included in the summary that appears on the initial pages of bank's annual report. You'll also hear it referred to as return on capital or return on net worth. It's the net income of the bank calculated as a percent of the total capital of the bank—common stock, preferred stock (if any), and retained earnings. Some supplement their capital position with subordinated debt (debt that, in the event of liquidation, would be paid out after other creditors of the bank were paid in full). Don't include any subordinated debt in your calculation. The capital figure you're after is usually labeled "Total Shareholders' Equity," or words to that effect.

In most banks, ROE falls in the 10-to-15-percent range, although all banks would like to be in the 15-to-20-percent range. Stay away from any bank with an ROE of under 10 percent if it's been at this level for several years. This ratio is very important to investors, but for you as a potential borrower from the bank, it's a good cross-check on the ROA. Large capital positions often lead to fine ROA's and not-so-fine ROE's, and vice versa. For example, you'll find that some of the big money-market banks have pretty poor ROA's—six-tenths of a percent or so—with ROE's in the 15-to-20 percent range.

But don't be misled by a good ROE if there is no capital. Once capital becomes minuscule, as it has for many savings-and-loan associations, it doesn't take much profit to produce a handsome ROE. The section below on quality of earnings goes into this point in more detail.

Capital Ratio

Another measure of a bank's financial strength is something called *capital adequacy.* In simplest terms, capital adequacy measures a bank's financial capacity to suffer losses from bad loans or poor investment choices and continue functioning as a bank. Capital adequacy is generally expressed as a ratio of capital (principally common stock, preferred stock, loan loss reserves, and certain types of subordinated debt) to total assets. What this ratio measures is leverage. Generally, banks with high financial leverage (or a low ratio of capital to assets) will experience more earnings volatility than banks with adequate capital. This condition may result from having too many risky loans, a high loan concentration in a few business sectors, excessive interest rate risk, or a combination.

Since 1992 a capital-to-assets ratio of 8 percent (or $8 in capital per $100 in earning assets) has been the standard measure of capital adequacy in banking. This is an international standard, adopted by banking regulatory agencies in the United States and 11 other industrialized nations. In addition, the amount of capital reserves is pegged to the probability of loss in each asset category, varying from a zero percent capital weighting for U.S. Treasury securities to 50 percent for single-family residential mortgages and 100 percent for commercial loans.

This *risk-based capital* formula has recently been updated, with the intention of providing depositors and investors a more accurate picture of the true credit risk in a particular bank's loan portfolio. Under the revisions to the international risk-based capital formula, regulators might require capital of more than 100 percent for some riskier types of loans, and for the first time, the banking regulators would use credit ratings of private sector credit rating agencies in calculating country risk and the loss probabilities of loans to international borrowers.

Persistent low capital, whether caused by rapid loan growth, above-average loan losses, or poor earnings, is always a cause for concern. If it's the last, you should steer clear of the bank. If the low capital position is caused by rapid growth, and you can confirm that by looking at one or two prior annual reports to shareholders, it's not likely to be caused by acquisitions, since they require regulatory approval and the regulators of commercial banks normally won't allow mergers unless the resulting financial institution is properly capitalized.

QUALITY OF EARNINGS

The three ratios just discussed give you a pretty good picture of the health of the bank you're considering. But to be on the safe side, you should take a look at the quality of the earnings as well. Sometimes earnings are not quite what they appear to be. There are four factors to focus on. In order of their appearance on the income and expense statement, they are: net interest income, provision for loan losses, securities gains, and unusual or extraordinary items.

Net Interest Income

Net interest, the single largest chunk of income for a bank, has two major components: the interest income the bank earns on all the loans and investments it owns, and the interest expense it incurs on all of deposits, certificates of deposit, and money that it borrows outright. This figure, calculated as a percent of total assets, should be around 4 or 5 percent. As a rule, any bank whose net interest income is less than 3 percent of its total assets is headed for trouble. If you were to look at the financials of a failed bank, you'd probably find very poor net interest income figures going back several years.

Another telltale you might find on statements indicating low net interest income is a line indicating that assets are being sold at a profit. All banks do that from time to time, but the profits so gained shouldn't be the difference between a black and a red bottom line. Doing that on a year-in, year-out basis is no way to run a bank, but you'll find that it's been done for many years preceding the failure of a bank.

Provision for Loan Losses

The provision for loan losses is the way a bank replenishes its loan-loss reserve, which is reduced whenever a bank has to charge off a bad loan. Charging off a bad loan doesn't directly reduce a bank's earnings, but making a provision for the loan-loss reserve does. If the accounting involved in these transactions sounds difficult, it might help to liken a bank's loan-loss reserve to the gas tank in a car. Just as a tank empties as you operate a car, a bank's reserve empties as the bank incurs losses on the loans it has made. The bank "fills up" its reserve by making a provision to the loan-loss reserve. That transaction, by the rules of accounting, reduces the bank's earnings and increases its reserve.

Wouldn't using the actual charge-off figures, instead of the loan-loss provisions be simpler and more to the point? The problem with this approach is that charge-off figures are difficult to locate—or are not provided—on many annual reports. The provision for loan losses, on the other hand, is clearly shown on virtually all statements. Over the long haul, charge-offs and loan-loss provisions should average out to about the same thing, though in any one year, either one of them can be larger than the other.

Charge-offs or loan-loss provisions in excess of three quarters of a percent of loans outstanding are high. If they're up around the 1 percent level and have been there for two or more years, they're a sign of lasting problems. One-half percent of loans outstanding is where a lot of banks find themselves these days, and no bank is ever happy about being there. One quarter of a percent is a good place to be, and less than that should be a warning to you. Why? Because, to carry things to an extreme, if a bank has no loan losses at all, then it is turning down not only all the bad loans, but a number of the good ones as well. Unless you have gilt-edged credit, you may find it tough to get the loans you need at this bank.

Securities Gains

The next item to look for is securities gains. This is usually one of the captions under an item called "Other Income." There are times when a bank's profitability is due largely to profits made by selling securities out of its portfolio. There's nothing wrong with this practice, but these profits should not be a major factor in the overall profitability of the bank for several years in a row. If they are, you have reason to be cautious about the quality of the bank's earnings.

Extraordinary Items

The last of the four major clues to quality of earnings is extraordinary items—sometimes called "unusual items," or a similar-sounding name. When it does appear on a bank's profit-and-loss statement, it can be found either just before the final net-income figure or under Other Income as a separate item. If you don't find it, it may be because it's been merged with another item. By definition, extraordinary items shouldn't appear regularly on a profit-and-loss statement.

CALL REPORTS

Call reports are an excellent source of statistical information about commercial banks and thrift institutions. Every FDIC-insured bank files a quarterly "Call Report" (officially a *Consolidated Report of Condition and Income*) with their appropriate banking regulator. Savings and loans and other thrift institutions file a similar report, the Thrift Financial Report (TFR). Call reports disclose a financial institution's status, including total loans and deposits, as of the last day of every quarter. Copies of call reports filed by banks and thrift institutions can be obtained from the FDIC's web site (*www.fdic.gov*).

Back to the Grapevine

As was suggested earlier, the grapevine can be a good source of information. Use it to follow up on some of the insights your financial-statement analysis has turned up. Many people in a town's business community are aware of the status of local banks.

Another good source of information are local stockbrokers, even if the bank isn't listed on the American or the New York Stock Exchanges or on NASDAQ. Many brokers follow the local business scene closely. Usually, when bank shareholders try to move stock, they check with local brokers first. While you're in the broker's office, it wouldn't hurt to buy some shares in the bank you're considering, just to get yourself on that bank's mailing list for quarterly and annual reports.

SAFETY AND SOUNDNESS RATINGS

While the FDIC does not release its ratings on the safety and soundness of banks and thrift institutions to the public, a number of organizations prepare safety and soundness ratings of individual banks and thrift institutions. Some also provide peer group rankings comparing similar size financial institutions.

Bank rating firms typically assign a grade or numerical score using an analytical formula. These assigned rankings are meant to indicate a covered institution's financial strength and ability to protect depositors' funds. Rating firms compute their evaluations from the same criteria—capital, assets, management, earnings, and liquidity—that bank examiners review during scheduled examinations of insured financial institutions.

Among the best-known and most widely available bank rating services are the following:

Bauer Group
P.O. Drawer 145510
Coral Gables, Florida 33114-5510

IDC Financial Publishing
P.O. Box 140
700 Walnut Ridge Drive, Suite 201
Hartland, Wisconsin 53029

LACE Financial Corp.
118 North Court Street
Frederick, Maryland 21701

Sheshunoff Information Services
P.O. Box 13203, Capitol Station
Austin, Texas 78711-3203

SNL Securities
P.O. Box 2124
Charlottesville, Virginia 22902

Thomson Financial Bankwatch
61 Broadway, Third Floor
New York, New York 10016

Veribanc
P.O. Box 461
27 Water Street
Wakefield, Massachusetts 01880

CHAPTER PERSPECTIVE

Whether you're a depositor, a borrower, or both, you should take a quick look at the overall health of your bank. An unhealthy bank is going to either fail or change its ways. If you're a borrower at this bank, either of those events could be dangerous to your own financial health. On the other hand, if you are a depositor at the bank and your deposits amount to less than one hundred thousand dollars, failure of the bank will probably mean little more than a possible reduction in the interest you earn.

Deposit Accounts, Balances, and Account Analysis

INTRODUCTION AND MAIN POINTS

This chapter discusses the different types of deposit accounts banks offer their customers, the rates and fees that go with those accounts, and the contents of a typical account analysis.

After studying the material in this chapter:

■ You'll have a better understanding of the range of accounts offered by banks.

■ You'll have some idea of the prices banks charge for deposit-related services and activities.

■ You'll know the difference between ledger, collected, and available funds.

■ You'll understand the concept of compensating balances.

■ You'll know how to review an account analysis and satisfy yourself as to the validity of the charges levied by the bank for the services it has rendered.

TYPES OF ACCOUNTS
Checking Accounts

Generally speaking, banks are not permitted to pay interest on the balances in business checking accounts. The primary exceptions to this rule are accounts of business partnerships and "not-for-profit" organizations (generally, charitable organizations provided for under IRS regulation 501c but not including certain not-for-profit corporations such as hospitals). If you seek this exception, you will be required by the bank to prove your company's eligibility.

Both business and personal checking accounts are referred to in banking regulations as NOW or transaction accounts. Some banks use that terminology; others use a wide variety of names, coupling them with an almost bewildering variety of features. You cannot generalize about the names and features but must ask each bank which features apply to each account. Even more important, you must ask about the pricing of various features, as well as the prices for different kinds of account-related activities, such as overdrafts and payments against uncollected funds (explained below). Some accounts, especially personal accounts, are described as free when in fact they trigger charges which make them anything but. In short, when you're looking for a bank to use, assume nothing, ask questions, and gather and read brochures at every opportunity.

Although banks may not pay interest on business checking accounts, most businesses can achieve much the same thing by having their accounts placed on an "analysis" basis. Under such an arrangement, the bank gives the customer an earnings credit for most of the interest income it earns on the average balances left in the checking account. The bank then offsets against those earnings all the costs incurred while servicing the account during the period in question. A report, or account analysis, detailing all the earnings and expenses on the account is sent to the customer at each period end, usually each month. Account analysis reports are discussed in detail later in this chapter.

When you're looking for a bank, be sure to consider some small ones. Some small banks don't charge aggressively, either because they don't have the detailed knowledge and ability to break down account activities into their various cost components or because they are reluctant to charge and perhaps offend their customers, although they may levy charges for a few activities such as overdrafts and special statements.

If, however, you're going to be a borrowing customer, it's usually far more important to select a bank based on the way it will handle your borrowing requirements than on the way it will charge you for its other services. Your search for a good commercial lender will probably lead you toward a larger bank, increasing the likelihood that your bank will be in a position to analyze your account and charge you for all the activity you incur.

Savings Accounts

Any business is permitted to keep a savings account with a bank. Interest-bearing deposit accounts, including savings accounts, pay a yield determined by the length of time funds are deposited and the posted rate of interest. By law, the yield is expressed as an Annualized Percentage Yield (APY), which is meant to help comparison shopping rates at competing financial institutions. The APY is calculated according to a formula that assumes the funds will be left in the account for a full 365-day year. Actual interest earned will be less if frequent withdrawals are made or funds are deposited for less than a year. This requires frequent trips to the bank, making it a cumbersome, inconvenient, and inflexible approach to funds management. Sooner or later, even the sleepiest of banks will notice the high (for a savings account) activity level and bring it to a halt. In short, savings accounts are not a very attractive option for businesses. A money market deposit account is similar to a savings account but usually pays a slightly higher rate of interest. Depositors are legally limited to six transfers or withdrawals per month, only three of which may be by check. There's no limit, however, on the number of transfers in or out of the account as long as you come into the bank and do them at a teller window. While this "quasi-interest bearing checking account" may represent an adequate cash management solution for some firms, especially very small ones, it really is not a very good option for most companies.

Certificates of Deposit

Certificates of deposit pay higher interest rates than those offered for savings accounts and money market deposit accounts and higher than the earnings credit used by banks in their account analyses. Under normal conditions, the longer the maturity of the CD, the higher the rate it will bear. Maturities range from thirty days to five years or more; six months is the most popular maturity by far. Unlike savings account rates, which change only rarely, the rates on certificates of deposit change daily at some banks and weekly at many others. Many banks have a special phone number you can call in order to learn their latest rates.

Rates for certificates of deposit larger than $100,000 run 1/2 of 1 percent to 1 percent higher than those with the same maturity but for smaller amounts. Remember, though, any deposit in excess of $100,000 in any one bank is not covered by deposit insurance.

Because certificates of deposit bear higher interest rates than traditional savings vehicles, they can be an excellent parking place for temporary funds. However, they can be difficult to work with because they have definite maturity dates; for a maximum return, the maturities have to match neatly with a company's cash flow needs. Bank regulations used to impose a penalty on money withdrawn from a certificate of deposit before maturity; although those regulations no longer exist, many banks still charge withdrawal penalties. Some of the penalties are punitive, while others are high enough to serve as deterrents aimed at reducing the paperwork or preventing depositors from getting long-term rates on deposits which turn out to be short term. Either way, the penalties can significantly reduce the return on your deposits, making it mandatory for you to use good cash management techniques if you are going to try to maximize company earnings by putting excess funds in CDs.

HR-10s, IRAs, and SEP Accounts

HR-10 accounts (sometimes referred to as Keogh accounts) are the account part of HR-10 retirement plans that allow self-employed individuals to make tax-deductible contributions (up to 25 percent of earned income, or $30,000) to the plan that are invested without incurring taxes until distribution at some later date. The two principal tax advantages of such plans are that individual contributions to the plan may be deducted from that person's gross income for tax purposes and that earnings on the accumulated contributions are not subject to income taxes while they remain in the plan. There is, of course, a day of reckoning, since those contributions and earnings do become subject to taxes years later when they are distributed from the plan.

HR-10 accounts can be opened at any bank, but because of the rules and regulations that govern such accounts, they very often are lodged in the trust department of a bank rather than in the retail area. They can be an important fringe benefit and therefore an important part of your efforts to retain valued employees. However, they, like the SEP accounts mentioned below, must comply with numerous IRS rules and regulations in order to qualify for their nontaxable status and shouldn't be undertaken without expert guidance.

IRA accounts are usually personal, rather than company, accounts; the exception is the so-called Simplified Employee Pension (SEP) account. A SEP account enables an employer to make contributions to an employee's retirement income by contributing amounts to employee IRA accounts. There are IRS rules that govern these accounts; if you make contributions for one employee, you must do so for all; your contributions can't exceed $30,000 per year or 15 percent of any employee's salary; and you can't discriminate in favor of an employee who is a company officer, a stockholder with more than 10 percent of the company's stock, a self-employed individual, or a highly compensated worker. SEP accounts appeal to very small companies and are favored by some professionals, such as doctors and lawyers, who have small staffs for whom they wish to provide retirement benefits of some kind.

SPECIAL SITUATIONS
Overdrafts and Uncollected Items

Most customers create overdrafts only occasionally and usually as the result of a miscalculation, an oversight, or some event beyond the customer's control. That kind of thing is bound to happen, and does, even to bankers. What is surprising, especially to people new to the banking field, is how many bank customers incur frequent overdrafts in their personal or business accounts, even though often they have sizable deposits in other accounts in the bank.

Some banks or branches are quite tolerant of overdrafts; they simply pay them and then call the customers to request the funds needed to reimburse the bank. Although many banks charge up to $30 for each check paid in overdraft, many would be happy if they never had to deal with another overdraft; others are willing to handle the overdrafts because the charges are a source of extra income. Some banks even levy a punitive fee in the hope that it will discourage overdrafts completely.

Overdrafts cause many problems from the bank's point of view. One is that they are really interest-free loans for as long as the bank remains unreimbursed. Also, they are expensive to the bank because they require special handling. In addition, a permissive attitude toward overdrafts increases bank vulnerability to criminals, who can be quite good at penetrating bank defenses by imitating the behavior of normal bank customers. Furthermore, no bank, even if the customer is entirely wrong, wants its customers to experience the irritation many do feel as they attempt to straighten out an overdraft.

Uncollected items, such as checks that have been deposited in one bank but not yet returned to the issuing bank so the transfer of funds can be effected, resemble overdrafts in that they represent a payout by the bank of funds that it has not yet received. The nature and causes of uncollected balances are discussed later in this chapter. Uncollected balances are not normally a problem for those who carry extra balances in their accounts, but for those who haven't got the money to do so or who are trying to keep balances as low as possible, it is important to understand how uncollected balances arise and how they can be avoided.

Most banks generate a daily list of all the overdrafts and uncollected for the day. Those lists are given wide circulation within key areas of the bank and are not the kind of hit parade with which you want your name or your company's name associated. Normally, overdrafts and uncollected items are entirely preventable; if you wish to make a good impression on your banker, staying off those lists is a wise idea.

Large Cash Deposits
Banks are required to report cash deposits (by filing Currency Transaction Reports) in excess of $10,000 a day to any one account, regardless of how many branches or deposits have been used in the transactions. More and more banks, however, are acquiring the computer capability to do the job properly and are thereby helping the

government to zero in on organized crime and drug traffickers, at whom the regulation is aimed.

More recent changes in bank regulations require similar reporting of the use of cash in excess of $3,000 for the purchase of cashier's checks, money orders, traveler's checks, and bank checks. If your business is a generator of large amounts of cash, you should know that the bank will be preparing lengthy forms on each of your company's cash transactions.

THE DIFFERENT KINDS OF BALANCES

When your bank provides you with an account analysis, as described below, you'll find that it contains references to three different types of balances: ledger, collected, and available.

Ledger Balances

Ledger balances are the balance figures shown on your statement even though they include balances that don't really exist at that time because the bank holding your account has not had time to collect recently deposited checks from the issuing bank.

If your statement period ends the same day you make a deposit to your account, for example, your statement will show an increase in your balance equal to the amount of that deposit. The statement will not show that in fact that check was not delivered to the bank of account until after the close of business that day, so that the money represented by the check had not actually been collected as of the end of the business day. The deposit at that point is what is known as a ledger balance; until the funds are actually collected the next day, the deposit in your account is incapable of earning any interest for your bank.

Collected Balances

When you deposit a check into your account, it's normally not actually recorded as a credit to your account until that evening. Suppose that the check has been drawn on an account in the bank across the street from your own bank. Typically, during the evening of the day during which the deposit was made to your account, the two banks exchange all checks drawn on one another and received during the day. Any difference between the total of checks received by each bank is settled by debiting or crediting special accounts each bank keeps with the other. If there are more than just two banks in town, then it is customary for all of those banks to be involved in the check exchange.

Much the same result is achieved if all of the banks involved send their checks each day to the same correspondent bank or to the same Federal Reserve Bank. In that case, the correspondent bank or the Federal Reserve Bank makes all the necessary debits and credits to the accounts of the banks involved; at the end of the day, the balances in those accounts reflect the day's deposits and withdrawals. And even if they don't have the same correspondent banks or the same Federal Reserve banks, the same result can still be achieved— it just takes more banks, more exchanges of checks, and more time.

By the next morning, the bank of deposit, your bank, has had a chance to collect the check and therefore is able to earn interest on the balance. That balance, called a collected or a good balance, is money that the bank can actually invest, spend, or pay out as it chooses. Uncollected or ledger balances, on the other hand, are balances in name only.

Many banks do pay interest on a deposit beginning with the day of deposit, but they are actually paying interest for at least one day, maybe two, on money they haven't received. While "interest from the day of deposit" is a catchy slogan, it is also an expensive practice, and, as computer technology advances and becomes more affordable, more and more banks are acquiring the ability to defer payment of interest on deposits until the money is actually collected.

Despite the distances involved, over 90 percent of the checks deposited in one bank today are charged back to the bank of account just one day later. Therefore, you ought to be able to withdraw tomorrow nearly all the money you deposit today, assuming that the bank knows you and knows that, in the event any of those checks bounce or come back bad, your account balance will be large enough to absorb the bad check when it is charged back to your account (i.e., when the deposit is reversed). Virtually all of the rest of the checks processed each day are collected on the second day, so that, for all practical purposes, your deposits should be fully collected within two days of the day of deposit.

Available Balances

Available balances refers to that portion of the balance in your account after the collected balances have been reduced by an amount equivalent to the amount which the bank must maintain as noninterest-bearing reserves at the Federal Reserve Bank. The bank's reserve requirement is 12 percent of the total demand account balances for banks holding more than $40.4 million in such accounts and 3 percent for banks with total demand balances below that amount.

Available balances, or investable balances, represent the actual balances on which the bank can earn a return. The income earned from the investment of those available balances is typically used by the bank to offset the expenses incurred in the normal day-to-day operation of that account.

Deferred Funds

Funds that have been deposited in a bank but that the bank will not permit to be withdrawn for a period of time ranging from a few days to as many as 30 days are called deferred funds. In most commercial banks, balances are deferred on new accounts only, especially if the new account is that of someone unknown to the bank.

Banks follow the practice of deferring balances to minimize the likelihood of fraud or embezzlement. Many thieves have capitalized on the knowledge that it can take days for a bad check to come back through the system and be charged against the account in which it was originally deposited. That kind of delay, when it occurs, leaves plenty of time to make one or more cash withdrawals from an account opened with bad checks or for checks cashed locally to clear the bad account before the original bad checks come back through the check-clearing system.

Generally speaking, deferring balances on new accounts has been an effective deterrent to such schemes. But it impacts on and often offends good customers. Some banks have abused deferred availability by applying it to all deposits, denying funds for many days to customers who were really entitled to them within a day or two. Except in the case of new accounts, deferred availability is not a practice to be condoned.

Since 1990, availability of funds may not be deferred for more than two days for local checks or more than five days for nonlocal checks. Funds availability regulations also recognize the new-account problem and do not limit restrictions on availability of deposits into new accounts for the first 30 days, with the exception of treasury and government checks and cashier's checks.

Compensating Balances

Banking charges for a variety of services are often paid by keeping a specified balance in a checking account, as opposed to having the bank deduct payment from your account for each service provided. This *compensating balance* offsets the bank's cost of servicing your account relationship. The compensating balance method of payment is common in cash management services. (See Chapter 6 for more about cash management.) If you negotiate a bank loan or line of credit, you may have to keep part of the loan proceeds in a checking account. The compensating balance is the cost of maintaining that credit availability. In exchange for keeping part of the loan in your checking account, you may get a break in the interest rate charged on the loan.

Do you have to maintain a compensating balance? When you deal with banks, there's no free lunch; if your account relationship incurs a servicing cost, you will probably pay for it one way or another. You can compensate your bank in one of three ways: keep a balance in your checking account, pay service fees, or pay with a combination of a balances and fees. Most banks are indifferent to the payment method, as long as they are adequately compensated. Some may charge a premium if you choose to pay by fee, but fees are often the least costly form of compensation.

Be wary of leaving too large a balance. Many small businesses keep excess balances in their checking account, a costly mistake. Your banker will never complain, but it's poor cash management and it's hurting your business. To find out whether you're leaving too much money at the bank, you must ask your banker to provide a monthly account analysis statement.

ACCOUNT ANALYSIS
A Typical Account Analysis

The account analysis statement is your bank's statement of services it provides for your business and how you paid for those services. The statement lists the services you used during a month, the bank's charge for each service, the minimum balances required to maintain your account relationship, and the balances required to pay for bank services. Remember that your account analysis statement is different from an account statement, which is just a monthly statement of account activity in a checking or savings account.

Generally, the account analysis statement has three principal sections: the first section lists ledger balances converted to available balances, the second section details all the bank services used during the month, the final section summarizes the information in the report. Figure 5-1 shows how the first part might look. Some banks also include the FDIC (Federal Deposit Insurance Corporation) charges for deposit insurance.

The ledger balance, as we defined it above, is the result of the entries made on the bank's books each day. Though there are no adjustments shown in our example, space is provided so that the average can be adjusted if, for example, an erroneous debit or credit has been made to the account and then corrected a few days later. Without the adjustment, the average for the month would be distorted by the lower or higher ledger figure.

FIGURE 5-1 *Account Analysis for the BBL Corporation*

Average ledger balance	449,252
Adjustments	0
Adjusted ledger balance	449,252
Less: average float	390,308
Average collected balance	58,944
Less: required reserve @ 12%	7,073
Average available balance	51,871
Earnings credit on average available balance @ 6.95%	300.42

The average float figure is the number of days each check was uncollected (usually just one day) multiplied by the amount of each check. The total represents the portion of the average ledger balance on which the bank was unable to earn interest. The figures in the example show that the company took money out of its account almost as quickly as it put money in, with the result that there was a net average of only $58,944 remaining at the end of the month.

The next entry deals with reserves the bank is required to keep at the Federal Reserve Bank. Since the bank can't earn any income on that part of the balances which the company leaves with the bank, an amount equivalent to the reserve, in this case $7,073, is deducted from the average collected balance in order to arrive at what is called the average available (or investable or usable) balance of $51,871.

The next entry on the account analysis converts the average available balance into an earnings figure, using the rate of 6.95 percent. That percentage, which is usually tied to some established rate, changes each month as rates in the marketplace fluctuate. Some banks may use such a rate as a guide without committing themselves to any particular rate or increment above or below that rate. The rate is an important figure in the analysis, and you should take it into account when you're comparing cost at different banks.

The final item in this portion of the account analysis, the earnings credit, is determined by applying the 6.95 percent figure to the average available balance figure. In the example used, the result, $3,605.03, is then divided by twelve since the average balance is on hand for only one month instead of a full year; some banks divide the $3,605.03 by 365 and then multiply that by the number of days in the month being analyzed.

The second section of the account analysis provides a detailed listing of the activities that took place in the account during the month. It is followed by the third section, which summarizes the entire analysis. Figure 5-2 shows how those last two portions of the statement might look.

FIGURE 5-2 *Account activity and summary*

Services	Number of Items	Price per Item	Activity Charges	Available Balance Required
Account maintenance	1	8.0000	8.00	1,381.29
Debits paid on account	246	.1300	31.98	5,521.73
Deposits made to account	31	.2500	7.75	1,338.13
Deposited items:				
Items deposited	1,142	.1100	114.20	19,717.99
Returned unpaid	13	5.0000	65.00	11,223.02
FDIC insurance assessment	449	.0833	37.40	6,457.55
Total activity charges			264.33	
Total available balance required to support account activity				45,639.71
Average available balance				51,871
Difference			36.09	6,231

The total dollar charge for each type of activity is divided by the allowable interest rate, 6.95 percent, thus producing a dollar amount that would earn an amount equal to the total charges for the activity. That amount is then multiplied by 12 in order to inflate the balance to the point where it can earn interest required in just one month since the period under analysis is only one month.

The account maintenance charge is levied by most banks to cover things like printing, postage, paper, and staff expense. The rest of the items, however, refer to specific activities. Debits paid on account are primarily checks written on the account, plus any other debits that might have been made to it. In the example, there were 246 debits, for each of which the analysis (not the account) was charged thirteen cents. There were 31 deposits to the account, including a total of 1,142 checks or other credits to the account. Thirteen of the checks were returned unpaid.

The final "activity" shown is the fee for FDIC insurance. All commercial banks are charged an assessment for FDIC deposit insurance provided through the FDIC's Bank Insurance Fund. This deposit insurance premium varies according to the FDIC's assessment of financial institution risk. In general, well-capitalized banks (banks meeting or exceeding the 8 percent ratio of risk-based capital to total assets) pay a lower insurance premium than undercapitalized banks. Savings banks and savings and loan associations pay similar risk-based insurance premiums for deposit protection by the Savings Association Insurance Fund (SAIF). In 2000, the FDIC rate schedule for BIF deposit insurance was set at 0 to 27 basis points per year. The average insurance assessment was approximately 12 basis points, or $12 per $1,000 of deposits.

The figures in our example show that the bank earned more money on the account, using the 6.95 percent earnings rate, than it would have received had it charged the company directly for all the activity in the account. The bank made a profit, as the analysis shows, of $36.09, an amount that probably is lower than its actual profit on the account. For one thing, the bank probably earned more than 6.95 percent on the average available balance. In addition, the bank has presumably built into its price structure some element of profit, which should also be included in its overall profit.

The customer wound up with an extra balance of $6,231, while paying in full for the services it received by leaving idle balances in the bank. The extra balance becomes a nonearning asset for the company, meaning that, using the bank figure of 6.95 percent, the company, at least in theory, lost out on interest income of $36.09 for the month—certainly not a lot of money, but the customer should realize that if it had not run its account so closely, it could have wound up with a much larger nonearning balance and therefore a much greater loss.

The company may decide to transfer more money out of the account in the following month so that when the two months are averaged together, the leftover balance will be close to zero. Many companies do just that; in fact, banks themselves do the same thing with the accounts they maintain at the Federal Reserve Bank.

Some banks permit customers to run negative average available balances, in which case the above suggestion works well. Other banks, however, assess a penalty rate of 5 percent or more above the earnings credit rate (6.95 percent in our example) on negative balances. This penalty may well be higher than the rate at which the company is borrowing money under its normal credit arrangements with the bank or more than the company can earn by investing the money. In such a case, the penalty rate makes negative balances an unattractive alternative for the company.

There is an almost endless list of bank services that can be performed for a customer and for which the cost is included in the account analysis. Banks charge different prices for different activities and some don't charge at all for some, so it is important that you do some comparison shopping from time to time to be sure you're being charged a reasonable and competitive price for the services you're getting.

The following list includes representative activities and prices you might find on a bank's price schedule:

Account maintenance	$12 per month
Checks paid (on us)	.20
Deposits	.40
Checks deposited	.12 each
Stop payments	20 each
Overdrafts	30 each
Returned checks	20 each
Deposited items returned unpaid	10 each
Wire transfers—incoming	15 each
—outgoing	20 each
Strapped currency supplied	.50 per $1,000
Coin supplied	.25 per roll
In-house transfer	5 each

The account analysis statement is the banking industry equivalent of an invoice. Banking is one of the few industries where the service provider can deduct its servicing costs from your account and then tell you how much you were charged. What can you do about it? You should monitor the account analysis statement each month. Track the account activity and service charges in your analysis statement using a spreadsheet program and compare activity from one month to the next, looking for discrepancies or changes in transaction volume and bank pricing. By tracking the information reported by your bank you can more easily detect variances or discrepancies. If you discover any variances, notify your bank immediately.

Every six months, you should review the account analysis file with the following objectives in mind:
- minimize your balances
- avoid any overdraft charges
- adjust your target balance if your account activity changes significantly
- eliminate any extra accounts and accounts where the account maintenance charge is higher than the value of the account.

Profitability Analysis

Computers have made it much easier for banks to have a clear picture of their profitability in specific areas, as well as a fairly good idea about the level of profits from the overall relationship with each customer. In some banks, the account analysis is only a starting point; the bank also analyzes rates on loans and deposits for each account, including personal loans and accounts and the costs of servicing all aspects of the relationship and then combines everything for one overall profitability figure. You would do well, if your bank compiles such data, to ask to see them.

CHAPTER PERSPECTIVE

In most cases, banks cannot pay interest on business checking accounts. Therefore, it is important that businesses not leave idle money in the bank. There are interest-bearing alternatives, such as savings accounts and certificates of deposits, but because of the high level of activity in most business accounts, it is difficult to estimate cash flows closely enough for such alternatives to be attractive parking places for excess funds.

The different kinds of balances that arise in the course of a normal banking relationship are the bank's primary source of reimbursement for the costs of servicing an account. The account analysis sets forth these prices and volumes of activity. That tool, coupled with proper cash management (the subject of the next chapter), makes it possible for businesses to achieve the equivalent of an interest-bearing checking account.

Compare the services your bank offers and its charges with those of competing banks. There's nothing wrong with negotiating with a bank over rates on deposits or loans or the price of various services. Banks are entitled to profits on the work they perform for you, but you may find that there's more room for negotiation than you realized.

Cash Management

INTRODUCTION AND MAIN POINTS

This chapter discusses how to manage your most important asset—your cash on hand—with some easy-to-apply financial management techniques. The objectives of cash management are the same regardless of business size: collect money from your customers as quickly as possible, disburse funds slowly (but within legal constraints and industry practice), and concentrate funds from multiple bank accounts so you can invest your funds safely and earn the best possible return on investment.

After studying the material in this chapter:

■ You'll know the most important areas to investigate to improve your cash flow.

■ You'll see how cash flow can impact your interest income and/or your interest expense.

■ You'll see how simple bank services can help you keep your noninterest earning balances at a bank as low as possible.

■ You'll begin to understand some of the short-term investments that are available to you now or that will be as your company grows in size.

COMPONENTS OF CASH MANAGEMENT

Cash management, also called funds management or money management, is all about improving the utilization of funds. Improper handling of cash costs money, but more important than that, your business itself may be at risk. Numerous studies have pinpointed lack of cash as the biggest single cause of business failures. A business reporting impressive growth in sales year after year may be headed for disaster if its ability to convert sales orders into cash falls much behind its revenue growth.

The principles of cash management (accelerating the conversion of receivables into cash and applying a disciplined approach in paying creditors and suppliers) can be effectively utilized in any business, regardless of company size or cash management sophistication.

Big companies spend millions of dollars a year moving money around the world and have access to cash management services beyond the reach of small businesses. But there is almost no correlation between company size and cash management expertise. Believe it or not, big companies sometimes make bad mistakes when it comes to managing their corporate cash.

MAXIMIZING YOUR CASH FLOW
Cash Flow Forecasting

Do you know your business income and expenses for the next three to six months? Most businesses don't take the time to try to forecast their cash position, so they're either cash poor or cash rich but don't know where they stand from one day to the next. They'll look at their daily cash balance, but that's about all they review. If cash poor, they borrow for much of the year to finance inventory and pay down debt as cash becomes available. Cash-rich companies, on the other hand, have adequate cash to cover day-to-day operating expenses. They could easily invest some of their cash surplus in short-term money market securities, and pick up some additional income, but only if they had a better idea of their cash requirements over the same time period.

The first step in maximizing your cash flow is preparing a cash budget so you can get a more accurate picture of cash inflows and cash outflows. Start by preparing a list of monthly income from regular sources, such as customer payments received by the payment due date, and a list of monthly expenses. Do the same the following month, and every succeeding month for the next six months. Once you have data for the first six months, your cash-flow budget worksheet makes it easier to project your business cash flow and expenses over the next six months or a full year into the future.

What you learn from this data collection exercise is important to your business. You will know whether your company is generating the necessary cash for business expansion. You can identify gaps in your cash flow, the months when cash outflows are exceeding cash inflows. Your analysis is also very useful when you apply for a bank loan; your banker will want assurances your business is generating enough income to repay the loan. Paying off any outstanding balance may be one of the conditions for getting the loan. If you are borrowing from an unsecured line of credit, your banker may require you to pay off the loan balance in full once a year—a "clean-up requirement," in bankers' parlance—to demonstrate your financial stability.

Most of the information necessary to prepare a cash-flow budget is readily available or can be estimated with reasonable certainty.

The due dates for payments to others are known in advance as are the dates when you expect to receive payments from customers with good payment records. By analyzing the collection pattern of your receivables, you can get a very accurate picture of your customers' bill-paying patterns. Some will pay 30 days from shipment, others within 60 days, and some after 90 days. This analysis helps you see the correlation between sales and receivables, and the time necessary to convert receivables into cash, which is very important in preparing a cash budget. If you offer trade discounts for early payment, say a 2 percent discount from the amount billed for early payment, be sure that discounts are properly taken.

On the disbursements side of the ledger, a thorough analysis of check-clearing times should give a fairly accurate picture of the actual dates when funds are debited from your checking account to pay suppliers and other creditors. It is important to remember that your checking account must have sufficient funds to cover payments to others when the checks are presented for payment, not the date when the checks were written. The table set out as Figure 6-1 shows what a cash-flow forecasting worksheet might look like.

Accounts Receivable

Accounts receivable, or money owed you by customers, is one of the primary consumers of company cash; no matter the reason for the delay, slow-paying customers cause you to lose interest income or incur interest expense.

You are also vulnerable to the customer whose company is failing and who ultimately goes out of business. When that happens, you lose potential interest income as well as all or part of your principal. In many cases, you might have avoided or minimized the loss by cutting off the company's credit.

It is important that you set up a system, automated or manual, which regularly provides you with a list of those who are taking too long to pay what they owe. Once you have the information, it's important that you act upon it, which can be particularly troublesome for smaller companies and for those who pride themselves on being "close to the customer."

Some computer programs for accounting can help generate the kind of information you need to stay on top of your receivables. As a rule, it's better to let your customers resolve their financial difficulties through their banks, rather than putting yourself in the middle by allowing them to delay paying their debts to you.

It's important to ensure that your customers are being billed properly for what you're selling them by doublechecking every bill

FIGURE 6-1 *Cash-Flow Budget Worksheet*

Cash-Flow Budget Worksheet

	January	February	March	April	May	June	Total
Beginning Cash Balance		$0	$0	$0	$0	$0	
Cash Inflows (Income):							
Accts. Rec. Collections							0
Loan Proceeds							0
Sales & Receipts							0
Other:							0
							0
Total Cash Inflows	$0	$0	$0	$0	$0		$0
Available Cash Balance	$0	$0	$0	$0	$0	$0	
Cash Outflows (Expenses):							
Advertising							0
Bank Service Charges							0
Credit Card Fees							0
Delivery							0
Health Insurance							0
Insurance							0
Interest							0
Inventory Purchases							0
Miscellaneous							0
Office							0

FIGURE 6-1 *continued*

Payroll							0
Payroll Taxes							0
Professional Fees							0
Rent or Lease							0
Subscriptions & Dues							0
Supplies							0
Taxes & Licenses							0
Utilities & Telephone							0
Other:							0
Subtotal	$0	$0	$0	$0	$0	$0	$0
Other Cash Outflows:							
Capital Purchases							0
Loan Principal							0
Owner's Draw							0
Other:							
Subtotal	$0	$0	$0	$0	$0	$0	0
Total Cash Outflows	$0	$0	$0	$0	$0	$0	$0
Ending Cash Balance	$0	$0	$0	$0	$0	$0	$0

before it goes out. If you don't, you're leaving yourself open to cleri-
cal errors that could shortchange both your cash flow and your
profits.

It's a good idea to review your bad debts, as well. Maybe you've
charged them off and gotten some tax relief out of them. But some of
those ex-accounts may not be as financially ill as you once thought
they were. They might even be able to pay off, or at least reduce,
however modestly, what you once thought was a bad debt. If you
haven't got the time or staff to run down such debtors, there are
agencies and attorneys who specialize in mining bad-debt lodes.

Night Drops and Cutoff Times

Many businesses make use of the night drops that most banks provide for those customers who wish to make their daily bank deposit
after normal banking hours. It's a convenient service and avoids having cash lying around overnight. But you will not get a deposit
receipt. If you're one of those businesses, you might consider, after
looking at the makeup of your deposits, whether it makes sense for
you to make part of that deposit earlier in the day. Total the bigger
checks in your deposit for several days and see what they average
out to for a typical day. Then multiply that amount by the interest
rate you're paying on your loan at the bank or by the interest rate
you're earning on your investments. If it's a significant amount for
you, even after allowing for the cost of sending someone to the bank
for an extra visit each day, all you need do to earn that money is get
that batch of checks down to the bank each day before cutoff time—
that time during the afternoon when the tellers close their books for
that particular day and then immediately open up again with everything seeming the same except that from that time on, everything
they process becomes part of the next day's work. That means that
any deposits you make after that time are credited to your account
one entire business day later, reducing your available balances and
resulting in more interest expense or less interest income.

Sweep Accounts

Sweep accounts are a convenient vehicle for moving surplus checking accounts funds, which don't pay interest, into a short-term
money market investment, usually on an overnight basis. The next
day, invested funds are redeposited in your account along with interest earned. Sweep accounts can be set up for almost any business;
some sweep programs will move as little as $500 into an investment
account.

If you have a sweep account, everything that's left in your account at the end of each day is invested overnight at a good return. In the morning, that investment is undone and the funds are returned to your regular account. The idea is to enable you to get your company's excess balances out of its noninterest-bearing checking account and into something that provides a decent return whenever possible.

If your sweep account is with a larger bank, one large enough to be issuing its own commercial paper, then your overnight investment may be placed in that bank's commercial paper. If you're with a smaller bank, your overnight investment is more likely to be in what is called a repurchase agreement, or repo, so called because your excess money, the money that has been swept out of your account, is used to purchase securities from the bank, which agrees to repurchase those securities from you the next day. Usually the securities are government or agency bonds already in the bank's portfolio. Both the purchase and the repurchase are done at the par value of the security. The interest you receive, however, is not normally the same as the interest rate on the securities but is at some increment over a popular or well-known rate such as the federal funds rate. The bigger the repo, the better your rate will be.

Amount of Sweep	Rate to Be Earned
Less than $100,000	Fed Funds rate less 1.75%
100,000–499,000	Fed Funds rate less 1.25%
500,000–1,999,000	Fed Funds rate less .90%
2,000,000 plus	Fed Funds rate less .75%

Thus, on a day when the fed funds rate is 8 percent, your excess balances earn anywhere from 6.25 percent to 7.25 percent—much better than letting those balances sit idle in a checking account.

There is, of course, a charge for such a service, varying from one bank to another but typically $100 a month. You should deduct that cost from the return you earn on your excess balances in order to calculate the net gain achieved over letting your money sit idle. For example, on an average investment of $100,000, the $100 a month amounts to a charge of 1.20 percent per year, which effectively reduces the return to just over 5 percent, a vast improvement over zero. The impact on a $2 million average invested balance is much less, an almost negligible .06 percent, making the service for that customer a much better bargain.

It might be argued that you can do your own investing and gain a better return than shown above. On the surface of things, that is correct. But there would also have to be a very considerable investment of time and effort in order to obtain daily rates and to juggle maturities of CDs, bonds, or other investments so that they mesh closely with your cash flow. Chances are good your skills might be better applied to other areas of your business.

This is not to say that you shouldn't look closely at the excess balances swept out every day. There may be monthly or seasonal patterns in your cash flow that enable you to skim money out of the account and out of the sweep program for a month or more and invest it at the higher rates normally associated with longer maturities in CDs, U.S. government paper, or other investments. That, too, takes time, but nowhere near what would be involved if you tried to do the whole sweep every day on your own.

You can pay for the sweep service, as with any other bank fee, either by paying directly or by leaving sufficient balances on hand for the bank to earn the fee by investing the balance for its own account.

There's a good reason to pay for this fee, and perhaps some others as well, by simply leaving balances in the bank. From time to time, even with the best of surveillance, the unexpected will occur in your account, with the result that your balances will be pulled down below the level left after the morning sweep is made. The result will be an overdraft *if* there's no pool of balances in the account to compensate for services rendered. Compensating by means of a balance, while a little more costly, provides a margin of comfort that may be worth the slightly higher cost.

If your bank doesn't offer sweep accounts, maybe the time has arrived for it to get into the sweep business. Many banks begin doing the sweeps manually, and your account might be just the right opportunity for your bank to add a new service that it can later offer to others. If your bank doesn't want to operate a sweep account, ask if any of its nearby correspondents do; sweep accounts have become quite commonplace, and you shouldn't have too much difficulty finding a bank that can do the job for you. Of course, you may be forced to change banks, something you need to evaluate in terms of the quality of your overall relationship with your current bank. There's always the possibility you'll be able to find a way of dividing your business between the two banks.

MONEY MARKET INVESTMENTS

Business checking account deposits typically do not earn interest. In order to get full advantage of money market yields it is usually necessary to concentrate funds in one location to maximize investable balances. Short-term money market instruments can be indexed off a bank's prime rate, the Federal Reserve discount rate or three-month, six-month or one-year treasury bill rates.

Commercial Paper

Commercial paper is a short-term, unsecured promissory note with a fixed maturity. Companies issue commercial paper, denominated in amounts of $100,000 or more, to raise working capital. The issuing company promises to pay the buyer of its commercial paper its face amount at maturity. Standard & Poor's and Moody's Investors Service assign ratings to corporations and financial institutions based on an ongoing review of their financial condition, management, back-up lines of credit, pledged assets, and financial guarantees.

Major investors in commercial paper are money market funds, insurance companies, corporations, bank trust departments, and pension funds. Maturities range from 1 day to 270 days. Commercial paper is typically issued in bearer form although book-entry issuance is becoming more common and is expected to eventually replace certificated commercial paper. Rates are quoted on an actual/360-day discount basis.

Bankers' Acceptances

A bankers' acceptance (BA) is a time draft or bill of exchange with a maturity of six months or less. The bank on which the instrument is drawn stamps the word "accepted" on the face of the draft and, by doing this, guarantees payment of the draft, regardless of whether the customer has repaid the bank. Bankers' acceptances are virtually unknown outside the money market, which is unfortunate because BAs are among the safest short-term investments available. Bankers' acceptances are issued in bearer form and are usually traded in round lots of $5 million, although odd lots as small as $25,000 are often available. Maturities range from 1 day to 180 days. Rates are quoted on an actual/360-day discount basis.

Repurchase Agreements

A repurchase agreement (repo) is created by the sale of a security with an agreement by the seller to repurchase at a later date at the same price plus interest. This arrangement permits the buyer (investor) to earn a return on a collateralized basis for a maturity matching the buyer's needs. Maturities range from 1 day (an overnight repurchase agreement) to 90 days.

U.S. Treasury Bills

U.S. treasury bills are short-term obligations of the U.S. government. Bills that mature in three months and six months are sold weekly. Bills with the maximum one-year maturity are auctioned every four weeks. T-bills are issued only in book-entry form and are sold at a discount, paying the face amount at maturity. T-bill rates are quoted on an actual/360-day basis. T-bills can be bought or sold for an initial minimum of $10,000 and in increments of $5,000 afterward. The secondary market for U.S. treasury bills is the broadest of all short-term money market instruments, because of their low credit risk, the variety of maturities and large volume of issues offered for sale to investors.

LOCK BOXES

A lock box, which literally short-stops checks in the mail, is a fine example of how to accelerate the flow of cash into your account. The idea is that you rent a post office box and give your bank access to it. The bank then picks up the mail in your box several times every morning, the actual number of pickups depending on mail deliveries, volume of work, and similar factors.

The bank opens envelopes from your box and removes the checks from them. It copies the checks, deposits the funds in your account, and then sends the checks on their way back to the banks on which they were drawn. The bank also prepares a daily journal showing all necessary details of each of the day's deposits, including dates and amounts. You are also provided with a worksheet that summarizes account activity for the day, starting with the beginning ledger balance and the deduction of float and then showing transfers made in and out of the account, application of funds to reduce borrowings elsewhere in the bank (or to increase borrowings, if needed), purchases and sales of repos, and the balances required to pay for the day's account activity.

The savings you achieve from a lock box depend on how long those checks might otherwise have lain idle in your office before they were brought down to the bank for deposit in your account. Multiply the dollar amount of incoming payments for a typical day by the number of days by which the deposit into the bank account is accelerated by use of the lock box; apply a current interest rate to that figure, and the result is the annual savings the lock box can produce for you.

A second advantage of a lock box is that it provides better and more-up-to-date knowledge of the overall status of your account. The bank not only delivers to you each day all the mail that came into the box, minus the checks, but normally advises you one or more times during the morning of the complete status of your account, enabling you to make timely decisions about how to fund the rest of your accounts.

There are some conditions that you should meet before establishing a lock box. First, there needs to be a sufficient volume of items to make it worthwhile to set up the process in the first place. Second, the items coming into the lock box ought to be fairly uniform. Ideally, there should be a low number of exception items, that is, items on which the check amount doesn't match the amount on the invoice or the remittal form that accompanies the check or on which there is some other kind of problem. Such items call for special handling and add to the overall cost of the lock box operation. If the invoices or remittal forms have pre-encoded MICR (magnetic ink character recognition, found at the bottom of virtually every check written today), it can speed up the process considerably and save on the costs to the company.

Lock box charges normally include a per month charge, really a maintenance charge, plus a charge for each item processed, ranging from 25 to more than 50 cents, depending on the nature of the processing involved. You also have to pay for the rental of the post office box. The bank will likely charge you for the cost of having someone pick up your mail and later deliver it to you along with the records for the day. That charge can come to $20 or $25 or more per trip, depending on costs and wage scales in your area. There may be additional charges as well, depending largely on the level of service you and your bank work out.

ZERO BALANCE ACCOUNTS

Zero balance accounts, frequently called ZBAs, are accounts with no balance in them until checks are presented to the account for payment. At that point, whatever money is needed to pay those checks is transferred from another company account, returning the balance in the ZBA back to zero after the checks are paid.

Payroll accounts provide a good example of how effective a ZBA can be. Years ago, many companies with separate payroll accounts fully funded those accounts each payday, leaving idle balances in the payroll account until all the employees' checks had been presented for payment, reducing the account balance back down to zero. After companies noticed that there were similar patterns of drawdown on these accounts each pay period, some company treasurers began to fund the accounts only partially on payday and then made additional deposits to the account on several subsequent days.

They thus enabled their companies to stay more fully invested by reducing and nearly eliminating a source of idle company balances.

The ZBA reverses the payroll process. It starts with no money at all and receives funding only when the account is hit with incoming checks. ZBA accounts are now used by many companies for other than payroll purposes, since they provide an excellent way of segregating types of payments, such as accounts payable and subsidiary or divisional disbursements, into as many separate accounts as company treasurers think they need.

Typically, when one or more ZBAs are set up, there is also a primary investment, disbursement, or funding account from which the monies will be funneled into the ZBAs as needed. The bank is likely to charge you a setup fee to get the arrangement up and running; from thereon in there will be the usual activity charges, including transfer charges, all of which are part of the expense of providing your company with a system that generates up-to-the-minute information on your cash needs or surpluses and that provides the flexibility needed to move in any direction suggested by the information received.

Account Reconciliation

Reconciling an account is probably one of the most tedious jobs for many bank customers, both personal and corporate. Many banks offer check reconciliation services to their business customers; the company need only provide the bank with a list of the check numbers for the checks issued during the reconciliation period. The bank in turn provides a detailed report listing all checks, in the order of their check numbers, paid during the period; the amounts paid, the date on which they were paid, and, if requested, data identifying payees. The report also shows which checks were unpaid at the date of the report and checks on which there are outstanding stop payment orders.

Normally the charge for a reconciliation service is a fixed amount per month, usually about $50, plus a per item charge of five or six cents an item. Most banks also offer, for a lesser per item fee, a sort service. No reconciliation is performed, but the checks are sorted numerically and then returned for the company to complete the rest of the process.

The Automated Clearing House

The Automated Clearing House (ACH) is an electronic payment and collection network developed years ago to reduce the burden of paper checks in the national payment system. While checks haven't

Tips for Cash Managers

1. Ask about deposit deadlines for same-day credit to your checking account. Remember that automated teller machine deposits after 3 P.M. lose one day's availability.
2. Consider eliminating little used or unnecessary banking services to reduce bank service charges.
3. If you have annual revenues over $100,000, maintain two checking accounts, using one to concentrate funds from subsidiary business units and a second checking account to pay creditors.
4. Monitor your monthly account analysis statement to detect changes in account balances and account service charges. If your bank is not sending this statement, ask for it.
5. Prepare an annual report card on your bank, rating service quality, pricing, range of banking services provided, and performance of your account officer.

disappeared from the scene yet, the ACH does handle a huge volume of transactions and has helped ease some of the check-clearing burden.

The first major use of the ACH was basically a consumer application and began in 1974, when the government initiated the direct deposit of Social Security payments into the accounts of recipients in banks all over the country. Many companies later began using the ACH network for direct deposit of employee payrolls. Other consumer applications include the use of preauthorized debits for the payment of recurring items, such as insurance premiums and mortgage payments, and for variable amounts, such as utility bills. A growing and more recent application is for point-of-sale transactions in which consumers authorize direct charges to their accounts while they're at the store counter.

As a cash-concentration tool, the ACH has largely replaced depository transfer checks—check-like instruments that facilitate the movement of funds from subsidiary accounts into a master account for purposes of fund consolidation. Today DTCs are used in the rare event when the deposit bank is not a member of an automated clearing house network. Federal legislation has given new impetus to using ACH payments as a preferred payment option. Since January

1999 federal government payments to government contractors must by law be channeled through the ACH network. The same rule applies to federal benefit payments, including Social Security benefits, paid to new beneficiaries.

CHAPTER PERSPECTIVE

It's expensive to tie up your money in assets you don't need. Excess cash is just as bad as excess inventory or excess receivables. Good cash management is a state of mind which aggressively routs out poor habits and lax management, seeks up-to-the-minute knowledge about the company cash position, and constantly looks for new ways to increase or speed up cash flow so that the company borrows less or invests more.

A good rule of thumb: if you're not hearing any complaints from your bank, you may be leaving too much cash there.

Trust Services

INTRODUCTION AND MAIN POINTS

This chapter provides a brief explanation of what goes on in a bank's trust department and ways some of these activities might be important to you or your business at some time.

After studying the material in this chapter:

■ You'll understand the importance of getting your personal affairs in shape if you're an owner or part owner of your business.

■ You'll learn of some of the trust instruments that can help you plan your estate.

■ You'll understand how a bank can assist you in preparing and maintaining some of your employee benefit programs.

■ You'll know what the trust department can do for you when or if yours becomes a publicly held company.

WHEN DO YOU NEED A TRUST DEPARTMENT?

As the manager of a small or medium-sized business, you will need a trust department when you decide to investigate or establish pension or profit-sharing plans for your employees. In addition, if your company becomes a publicly held company, a trust department can provide a number of services related to the issuance of stock, the maintenance of that stock once it's been issued, and the development and maintenance of shareholder relations.

There's also a personal reason for you to contact a trust department. If you are the owner or part-owner of a company, you ought to do contingency planning to protect your assets in case something happens to you. Your company stock is a normally highly illiquid asset with which your family may be ill-equipped to deal. Because of that, your heirs may not only have difficulty in resolving your estate but may well wind up with far less than they might have had you properly provided for them.

The easiest way to find a bank with a trust department is to ask your local banker. Many banks with total assets of $100 million or more have a trust department or at least a few people who provide trust services; the larger the bank, the more numerous and sophisticated those services will be. You can tell which banks have trust departments from their financial statements. Any trust income earned is shown on a separate line in the section on the income statement entitled Other Income. The Federal Deposit Insurance Corporation maintains a searchable database, accessible from its website (*www.fdic.gov*) of FDIC-insured and uninsured financial institutions that have trust fiduciary powers.

PERSONAL TRUST SERVICES
Living Trusts

A living trust is a legal entity you create to own property and use it for the benefit of someone else, either now or at some future date or event. It's called a living trust because it's something you create while you're still alive. The trust can terminate upon your death, or it can continue afterward if you wish and if you so stipulate in the trust.

Normally the living trust names a trustee, which can be you, a bank, an attorney, an accountant, or anyone else. Providing for a trustee can be a good way to bring in the kind of expert help administering the trust may require. A bank trust department, for example, can provide investment advice, records maintenance, safekeeping of securities, collection of dividends, and similar services, as well as make distributions of income and principal in accordance with the provisions of the agreement.

Living trusts can be irrevocable or revocable. The latter allows you to change trustees or to alter any other terms and conditions of the trust at any time you feel it's appropriate to do so. In short, living trusts are highly flexible instruments that enable you to provide for your family in the way you think best.

Testamentary Trusts

A testamentary trust is one created in a will; its provisions don't take effect until the maker of the will dies. A testamentary trust can:

- spare your surviving spouse all the business, financial, and investment responsibilities that are a normal part of your estate.
- protect your family from outsiders with dubious motives.
- provide financial supervision of bequests until your beneficiaries reach specified ages.
- provide financial support and maintenance for a physically or mentally incapacitated beneficiary.
- provide investment management and income collection for your surviving spouse.

▬ protect the estate and inheritance rights of your children and grandchildren.

Guardianship Trusts

A guardianship trust provides complete financial management for someone considered to be legally incompetent, such as a minor or someone who is mentally ill or deficient. A bank trust department can handle all income, such as Social Security, pension and veterans' benefits; pay all expenses, including medical and insurance bills, taxes, and food and clothing costs; and provide investment management for whatever funds are part of the trust.

Life Insurance Trusts

A life insurance trust can be established to provide funds upon your death to your estate so that the trustee or executor does not have to resort to a forced liquidation of trust assets because there are insufficient liquid assets available to meet pressing obligations, such as taxes. Other than maintaining the insurance policy, there are no trustee costs under a life insurance trust until you die; and, since it's usually a revocable trust, you can revise or refine it at any time in order to accommodate changes in circumstances. A life insurance trust also allows you to maintain full ownership rights on the policy during your lifetime.

Charitable Trusts

A charitable trust enables you to make a gift to a charitable organization and to claim that gift as a tax deduction while continuing to receive the income from the gift for yourself, or for others, for the remainder of the term of the trust. A charitable lead trust does much the opposite: it enables you to give the income to charity, thereby avoiding taxable income, even though the principal will be distributed to other beneficiaries at a later date. There are many other variations possible; all have much the same purpose—providing for yourself or someone else and reducing your tax burden while satisfying a desire to give to charity.

The Qualified Terminable Interest Trust (QTIP)

Assets that do not qualify for the marital deduction (a deduction for tax purposes for the value of all the property that passes from you to your surviving spouse) can be placed into a separate trust (sometimes called a QTIP trust, or a qualified terminable interest trust) with the provision that all of its income go to your spouse for as long as your spouse is alive and then go to other family members previously designated by you. In this way, the spouse receives the income needed while alive, and the remaining family members receive the assets after paying only one round of taxes instead of two, as they would if the unprotected assets were taxed first at your decease and then again at the death of your spouse.

Investment Management

You can open an investment management account with a trust department if you have assets that you can't give proper time and thought to. The trust department can take over full investment responsibility for you, if you wish, or leave that to you and handle only the custodial aspects of your assets, such as collecting dividends and other income, collecting matured or called bonds, selling or buying securities, investing in short-term funds, providing accurate tax records, safekeeping securities, and providing periodic reports on income and assets.

Some Critical Questions

The following is a list of questions to which you should give some thought, not only from the point of view of what's best for your business but also from the point of view of what's best for your family:

- What percentage of your business do you own?
- What is the fair market value of your interest?
- What is the tax basis of your ownership?
- Do you have any plans for disposing of your interest during your lifetime?
- How do you wish for your interest to be disposed of after your death?
    - transfer to your family?
    - sell to co-owner of business?
    - sell to a key employee?
    - sell to someone else?
- Is there a buy/sell or a redemption agreement?
- How and to whom do you want your assets distributed?
- If you and your spouse die prematurely, at what age do you wish your children to receive property?
- Do any of your children have special educational, medical, or financial needs?
- Is your spouse a good money manager?
- Do you wish to make any bequests to charitable organizations?
- If none of your children are living at the time of your spouse's death, to whom do you wish your estate to go?

It's not pleasant stuff to think about, but such questions do require careful consideration. Taking care of your family won't add a dollar to the bottom line of your company, but it might add considerably to your peace of mind.

EMPLOYEE BENEFIT SERVICES

The trust department of a bank can help you with pension plans of all sorts, including pension plans, profit-sharing plans, 401(k) salary deferral plans, Employee Stock Ownership Plans (ESOPs), and HR-10 plans. While such plans have many similarities, each has points of distinction and varies from company to company. Your bank's trust department can not only help you define your needs and those of your employees but can help you plan objectives, set up the plan, invest the funds as they come in, take custody of the securities in which you invest, maintain participant records, make payments to participants, and provide proper accounting for all of the plan's activities.

Types of Pension Plans

You can establish pension plans that call for fixed contributions each year by the company; plans can be also designed to provide the same benefit year in and year out to the beneficiaries.

Profit-sharing plans are a variation of pension plans but provide flexibility to your company since, under such a plan, the company does not have to make payments into the plan unless it has sufficient earnings. Payments may be limited to a certain percent of earnings, for example, with perhaps no payments required if earnings aren't at least a certain amount.

A 401k plan (often called a salary-reduction plan, because it reduces the amount of a participant's salary subject to income taxes) allows participants to invest untaxed dollars in a plan whose earnings are not subject to taxes until the funds are withdrawn years later.

An HR-10 plan (sometimes called a Keogh plan) is for a self-employed individual, or for employees who work more than 1,000 hours a year. HR-10s can be defined or fixed, contribution or defined benefit plans. In either case, contributions by any participant may not exceed $30,000 or 25 percent of earned income.

An ESOP is a trust that receives contributions from the company and invests them in company stock, thus giving employees a share of the ownership of the company. Contributions by the company are tax deductible up to 25 percent of the total payroll. Stock ownership can provide a real motivational plus for employees; the downside is that declines in stock values can be detrimental as well.

Investment and Administrative Services

Running any of the plans described in the preceding section can involve considerable time and responsibility, and turning to a trust department or some other source of outside help usually makes good sense. The investment responsibilities alone are significant and deserve the best professional help you can get. Larger trust departments have significant investment capabilities and should be asked, along with any others you might wish to invite, to bid for the opportunity of handling the investments of your employee plans. Similarly, the administration of employee plans is a complicated and detail-oriented operation. Many bank trust departments do a good job in this area as well and should be among those who are invited to bid for the opportunity of performing such work for you.

As your company grows, the likelihood that it will need some or all of these services will also grow. These plans are all complicated enough so that it would be entirely appropriate for you to start your comparison shopping on these products several years before you actually expect to put them in place.

SHAREHOLDER SERVICES

It may be a long time before your company gets to the point where it can go public, but when you do get there, you'll find that the trust departments of banks in large cities will be eager to help, not only with the process of going public but also in such roles as registrar and transfer agent for your stock. They'll also be interested in handling your dividend distribution and reinvestment programs and will offer you stockwatch services (to see who's buying your stock), odd-lot buyback programs (to cull out the smaller shareholders), and a host of other programs to help you with your shareholder relations.

CORPORATE TRUST SERVICES
Bond Trusteeships

Many trust departments act as trustee, registrar, and paying agent for bond issues put out by municipalities or corporations for a variety of purposes. Bank trust departments look out for the interests of those who purchased the bonds; if the bonds are financing the construction of a project, the trust department monitors the project to see that the funds raised through the bond sale are spent in accordance with the bond issue's terms. The trust department also pays out interest to bondholders as required, keeps track of the ownership of the bonds, and monitors bond calls (early redemptions) whenever they're provided for in the issue.

Escrows

Bank trust departments also act as escrow agents whenever two parties have something of value which needs to be held by a neutral third party until negotiations or a transaction can be completed. Mergers and acquisitions of companies, for example, sometimes provide escrow opportunities for a bank trust department.

CHAPTER PERSPECTIVE

The trust department of a bank is not likely to add much to your bottom line until you get large enough to use some of its corporate services for employees and shareholders. Still, if you're a goal-oriented company, it's never too early to start thinking about some of the services offered by a trust department so that when the time of actual need arrives, you'll be ready.

On the other hand, from a personal point of view, the sooner you get in touch with the personal trust area, the better. Putting your personal affairs in order should be a high priority for you, especially if you're the owner or part-owner of your company. Failure to plan your estate can tie both your company and your family into knots. Ask your local banker to put you in touch with a trust department near you, or talk to your accountant. Don't let the ease with which this task can be postponed prevent you from getting it done. You, your family, and your company deserve better.

International Banking

INTRODUCTION AND MAIN POINTS

This chapter discusses what the international department of a bank can do for you.

After studying the material in this chapter:

■ You'll learn where to get the international banking advice you need.

■ You'll learn what's involved in assuming foreign currency exchange risk or country or political risk.

■ You'll learn how drafts are used to help protect your sales or purchases.

■ You'll have an understanding of how export letters of credit and standby letters of credit work.

■ You'll learn some of the differences between an import and an export letter of credit.

■ You'll learn about the collections process and how it can protect your interests.

■ You'll understand how international payments are made.

DEVELOPING INTERNATIONAL TRADE

Although there are differences in the way some things are done in international trade compared to domestic business, once you learn the basics, the risks are not at all unlike those of conducting business in this country. There are, however, two added risks: foreign currency exchange risk and country risk. Your local banker can direct you to the international department of a regional or money center bank which is knowledgeable about the countries and currencies in which you are interested. Even if your bank is one of those large enough to have its own international department, your local banker will almost certainly have to refer you to the appropriate people in the bank's international department. Experts, one of whom will be a member of the international department of a bank, can help you understand the countries and the currencies with which you may be dealing.

After some general comments, the remainder of this chapter will be divided into three sections. The first and largest section is written for the companies in the United States that sell goods abroad. We will always refer to such companies as the exporter. The second section is written for companies in the United States that import goods into this country; we will always refer to such companies as the importer. The third section, a brief one, focuses on banker's acceptances.

Finding a Bank with an International Department

Most banks, even those with assets over $1 billion, don't have an international department because they don't have many customers interested in selling or buying overseas. However, your local bank can put you in touch quickly with one or more banks that are thoroughly experienced in the international field. If you're near a city that has offices of foreign banks, you might consider trying a bank from the country in which you're interested. Normally, though, until you're well established in the international world, you'd probably do better to stock with one of the domestic banks; you have more clout and connections, however modest, than you would have if you tried to work through a foreign bank. This applies not only while you're learning about conducting business abroad but after you've begun to export or import and may need to straighten out things that have gone wrong.

You might also try talking to officials at one or more large companies that conduct business in the country or countries in which you're interested. The treasurer of such a company may be able to arrange for you to talk with other people who are knowledgeable about the country you wish to learn about and may also be willing to arrange an introduction for you to an international banker. It would be hard to overemphasize the value to you of discussing the country in which you're interested with people who are already doing business there.

Credit Information

One of the difficulties you'll find in dealing abroad is the inadequacy of credit information. You may never know more about your customer or prospect other than that the prospect's bank regards the company as "satisfactory." The bank might even add that it has had good experience with the company. But that's about it. No financial statements, no Dun & Bradstreet reports, none of the detail which makes it a little easier to decide whether to extend credit to a company in the United States. If you're fortunate enough to receive some financial figures, chances are good they'll be in a format different than that used in the United States and that they'll therefore be rather hard to understand.

This means that, once you've got the "satisfactory" reading, you're going to have to rely heavily for the rest of your assessment of your customer on what you hear in your own business circles.

Trade Development

A little-known service of some banks is something referred to as "trade development." At its core is a bulletin that is circulated within the bank as well as to bank customers and prospects and that functions much like a "situation wanted" newsletter: "German manufacturer of widgets is looking for an outlet in U.S." or "French manufacturer desires source of widgets." When you begin working with your bank's international department, you might ask if it offers this service. It's a long shot, but it doesn't take much of your time and is certainly worth a try.

Letters of Introduction

Another little-known bank service is arranging introductions abroad to people who may be able to help make your trip more productive. First on the list is the banker and bankers with whom you will be working. Even if you don't think you're going to need a bank overseas, that local banker is in an excellent position to put you in touch with virtually anyone you want to talk to.

Foreign Currency Exchange Risk

As an exporter or importer, you need to be aware of the problems and dangers of dealing in foreign currencies. Currency values change daily, even by the minute, so that if you have foreign currency as one of your assets, you're adding an element of uncertainty to the figures on your balance sheet. There's nothing wrong with accepting payment in foreign currencies or agreeing to purchase in foreign currencies, but it's most important that if you do, you thoroughly understand the risks involved.

If you pay or are paid in foreign currencies, you can protect yourself against foreign currency exchange risk by entering into "spot" or "forward" contracts with your bank. These contracts are available in most convertible currencies and enable you to buy or sell foreign currency for delivery in one or two days (spot) or one or more months (forward). In a sense, each transaction is a bet by you that the exchange rate will be more favorable to you on the date you select than it is on the day you make the contract. More important, the contract fixes the dollar price or cost of the transaction and thereby eliminates further uncertainty for you.

You may decide that you'd be best off leaving the currency speculation to your customer or supplier or to your international bank. It's appropriate for you to want to be paid dollars for what you sell, and it's also appropriate for your customer abroad to want to be paid in the native currency. The resolution of those opposite needs is to let the banks do it through foreign exchange contracts or through letters of credit, discussed in the sections below.

The banks are the currency experts. They're the ones who actively trade currencies, adjusting their currency positions in accordance with what they think has happened, is happening, and is going to happen to each of those countries and their currencies. They're good at it (usually), they make money at it, and they're only too glad to be able to provide you with a service you need and want.

Country Risk

Country risk, according to a commonly accepted definition by international bankers, is any economic event, or series of events, resulting in nonpayment by private sector borrowers. The Asian financial crisis of 1997 and Russia's default on its bank debt in 1998, both of which led to serious balance of payment problems, were instrumental in leading the International Monetary Fund and others to a more inclusive definition of country risk.

International bankers can help you assess so-called country risk, another element in international trade. Countries are not much different from companies; they can be healthy or sick financially and need to be assessed just as carefully as any company you might deal with. There are countries with extremely high inflation rates, there are countries with no dollars available to spend on your goods, and there are countries likely to be taken over by a new political faction that may or may not honor the obligations of the preceding government.

When you agree to pay someone or to accept payment in a foreign currency, you are taking on not only the risk of fluctuating currency exchange rates but risks that arise from the economic and political condition of the country that issues it. That country, before you get paid, might undergo a revolution, might suspend or freeze all foreign currency payments, or might change its exchange rates. It's difficult enough to evaluate all the economic and political cross-currents in one's own country, much less those going on in other countries. There are countries in which, for decades, there has been virtually no country risk. Other countries, especially those with poor economies or raging inflation, are quite another story. You need all the help you can get if you want to properly assess country risk.

SERVICES FOR EXPORTERS
Drafts

Getting paid for a shipment abroad is somewhat different than getting paid for a shipment made at home. By the time your goods are placed on board a ship, cross the ocean, get unloaded, and clear customs, a considerable number of days will have passed. In the meantime, you, the exporter, no longer have documents to support your title in the goods, and you don't have payment. The collection process, whether or not it uses letters of credit (discussed below), is a means of maintaining your ownership or title in those goods until you either get paid or have firm assurance that you will in fact be paid at some future date.

There are a number of documents that you will probably be required to produce in order to complete your sale. Some of them are:

- commercial invoice
- consular invoice
- bill of lading
- insurance policy or certificate
- certificate of origin
- weight list
- certificate of analysis
- packing list

Whatever the particular documentation you and your customer agree on—and it could involve considerably more than the list above—you may forward it all directly to your customer upon shipment or, as is usually done, have it sent from your bank here to your customer's bank. An even better way, unless you and your customer have long experience and total confidence in each other, is to add one more document to the above list—a draft. A draft is a written order by the buyer, your customer, telling the overseas bank to pay you upon release of the necessary documents. This then becomes what is known as a "documentary" collection, and it can be done independent of, or in conjunction with, a letter of credit.

There are two major kinds of drafts: sight and time. With a sight draft, the accompanying documents are released to your customer immediately upon payment. A time draft, on the other hand, releases the documents only after your customer has accepted the draft, thereby agreeing to make payment in 30, 60, or 90 days, or some other previously agreed-upon period of time. By accepting the draft, the customer creates what is commonly known as a trade acceptance.

Either way, you wind up with no documents and a customer's promise to pay, either immediately upon receipt of the documents or at some previously agreed-upon date after receipt. Essentially, it's an open-account arrangement with your customer that is similar to the way most companies deal with their customers in this country: ship and then get paid within the agreed-upon time. The costs are minimal for both you and your customer and your customer needn't bother getting the bank to prepare a letter of credit with you as the beneficiary. If you've agreed to a time draft, then you've also provided financing for your customer. In addition, one of you will bear the foreign currency exchange risk, depending on whether the price you've agreed on is expressed in dollars or in your customer's currency. And you have political or country risk, which can be a matter of considerable concern for you, depending on the country in which your customer is located.

Letters of Credit

In many cases, you will be better protected by a letter of credit issued by your customer's bank than by the collection procedures just described. Your customer initiates the letter of credit with the foreign bank, and the overall cost to each of you will be more.

Letters of credit are available in a variety of formats. Some of the most common are: confirmed letters of credit, confirmed irrevocable letters of credit, acceptance letters of credit, or back-to-back letters of credit. Each type has a differing degree of bank commitment. In most import or export transactions, you will be dealing only with irrevocable letters of credit.

A letter of credit is just what its name suggests—a letter outlining the terms of an extension of credit. Typically, it is a letter from your customer's bank (usually called the issuing bank) to you. The letter is sent to a bank in this country and tells that bank to pay you the amount stated in the letter if you ship specified goods to your customer, as evidenced by the documents called for in the letter. Figures 8-1a and 8-1b illustrate two sample letters of credit and contain the kind of terms and conditions you'll have to meet in order to get paid.

With a letter of credit, your customer's bank has in effect substituted its credit for that of your customer. You still may not know much about your customer's financial health, and you probably don't know anything about the condition of your customer's bank either,

FIGURE 8-1a *Confirmed Letter of Credit*

MANUFACTURERS HANOVER TRUST COMPANY 1
LETTER OF CREDIT DEPARTMENT
4 NEW YORK PLAZA   NEW YORK, N.Y. 10015

DATE NOVEMBER 16, 1984
CONFIRMED IRREVOCABLE STRAIGHT
CREDIT

OUR NO.

ISSUING BANK NO

ADVISING BANK   214003   ISSUING BANK   L/C 100014

BANK OF ARGENTINA
BUENOS AIRES, ARGENTINA

BENEFICIARY   ACCOUNT PARTY
                                         HOSTIC INC.
TRUCKER NOVELTY LTD.   AMOUNT
136 MADISON AVE.   U.S.$105,000.00
NEW YORK, N.Y. 10012   EXPIRY DATE
                                         JANUARY 21, 1985

GENTLEMEN: WE ARE INSTRUCTED BY THE ISSUING BANK NOTED ABOVE TO ADVISE
YOU THAT THEY HAVE OPENED THEIR IRREVOCABLE CREDIT IN YOUR FAVOR.
AVAILABLE BY YOUR DRAFTS ON US AT SIGHT TO BE ACCOMPANIED BY:
  COMMERCIAL INVOICE IN TRIPLICATE.
  PACKING LIST IN DUPLICATE.
  FULL SET OF CLEAN ON BOARD OCEAN BILLS OF LADING CONSIGNED TO BANK OF
  ARGENTINA AND MARKED FREIGHT COLLECT AND NOTIFY BUYER.
  CERTIFICATE OF ORIGIN IN TRIPLICATE.

COVERING: ELECTRIC ADAPTERS, MODEL #2714, PURCHASE
     ORDER #2236, F.O.B.

DRAFTS AND DOCUMENTS MUST BE PRESENTED TO US WITHIN 10 DAYS AFTER THE
BILL OF LADING DATE, BUT WITHIN THE VALIDITY OF THE CREDIT.

SHIPMENT FROM NEW YORK TO ANY ARGENTINIAN PORT.

PARTIAL SHIPMENTS PERMITTED. TRANSHIPMENT NOT PERMITTED.

EXCEPT SO FAR AS OTHERWISE EXPRESSLY STATED, THIS CREDIT IS SUBJECT TO
THE UNIFORM CUSTOMS AND PRACTICES FOR DOCUMENTARY CREDITS (1983 REVISION)
INTERNATIONAL CHAMBER OF COMMERCE, PARIS, FRANCE PUBLICATION NO. 400. ALL
DRAFTS MUST BE MARKED "DRAWN UNDER MANUFACTURERS HANOVER TRUST COMPANY
ADVICE NUMBER 214003 DATED NOVEMBER 16, 1984."
THE ABOVE MENTIONED ISSUING BANK ENGAGES WITH YOU THAT ALL DRAFTS DRAWN
UNDER AND IN COMPLIANCE WITH THE TERMS OF THIS CREDIT WILL BE DULY
HONORED ON DELIVERY OF DOCUMENTS AS SPECIFIED IF PRESENTED AT THIS OFFICE
ON OR BEFORE THE EXPIRY DATE INDICATED ABOVE. WE CONFIRM THE CREDIT AND
THEREBY UNDERTAKE THAT ALL DRAFTS DRAWN AND PRESENTED AS ABOVE SPECIFIED
WILL BE DULY HONORED BY US.

SPECIMEN
AUTHORIZED SIGNATURE

                                   CONFIRMED
                                   LETTER OF CREDIT

FORM 24303F 5 84

22   This exhibit is fictitious and is provided only as an example. The information contained therein reflects the terms and conditions
     of the Uniform Customs and Practice per International Chamber of Commerce publication #400 in effect as of October 1984.

although the chances are good that it's solvent. However, you're protected most fully by a confirmed letter of credit, in which the bank in this country commits to paying you if you perform—even if the foreign bank fails or the buyer fails, or both. (The U.S. bank in this case is referred to as either the "advising" or the "confirming" bank,

FIGURE 8-1b *Unconfirmed Letter of Credit*

MANUFACTURERS HANOVER TRUST COMPANY 1
LETTER OF CREDIT DEPARTMENT

4 NEW YORK PLAZA   NEW YORK, N.Y. 10015

DATE DECEMBER 12, 1984

CREDIT

OUR NO. 204001   ISSUING BANK   L/C 100024   ISSUING BANK NO.

JAPANESE BANK LTD.,
P.O. BOX 102
TOKYO, JAPAN

BENEFICIARY

UNISONIC LTD.,
608 INDUSTRIAL BLVD.
EATONTOWN, NEW JERSEY

ACCOUNT PARTY   FUMI LTD.,

AMOUNT   U.S.$106,050.00   EXPIRY DATE

JANUARY 10, 1985

GENTLEMEN: WE ARE INSTRUCTED BY THE ISSUING BANK NOTED ABOVE TO ADVISE YOU THAT THEY HAVE OPENED THEIR IRREVOCABLE CREDIT IN YOUR FAVOR. AVAILABLE BY YOUR DRAFTS AT SIGHT ON US TO BE ACCOMPANIED BY:

SIGNED COMMERCIAL INVOICE IN TRIPLICATE.
PACKING LIST IN DUPLICATE.
CERTIFICATE OF ORIGIN IN TRIPLICATE.
AIR INSURANCE POLICY OR CERTIFICATE IN DUPLICATE.
AIRWAYBILL DATED NOT LATER THAN DECEMBER 31, 1984, CONSIGNED TO FUMI LTD., MARKED FREIGHT PREPAID.

COVERING: ELECTRONIC COMPOSER UNIT, MODEL #6322, C.I.F.

SHIPMENT FROM NEW JERSEY TO TOKYO, JAPAN.

PARTSHIPMENTS NOT PERMITTED. TRANSHIPMENT NOT PERMITTED.

DRAFTS AND DOCUMENTS MUST BE PRESENTED TO US WIHTIN 10 DAYS OF THE AIRWAYBILL DATE.

EXCEPT SO FAR AS OTHERWISE EXPRESSLY STATED, THIS CREDIT IS SUBJECT TO THE UNIFORM CUSTOMS AND PRACTICES FOR DOCUMENTARY CREDITS (1983 REVISION) INTERNATIONAL CHAMBER OF COMMERCE, PARIS, FRANCE PUBLICATION NO. 400. ALL DRAFTS MUST BE MARKED DRAWN UNDER MANUFACTURERS HANOVER TRUST COMPANY ADVICE NUMBER 204001 DATED DECEMBER 12, 1984."
THE ABOVE MENTIONED ISSUING BANK ENGAGES WITH YOU THAT ALL DRAFTS DRAWN UNDER AND IN COMPLIANCE WITH THE TERMS OF THIS CREDIT WILL BE DULY HONORED ON DELIVERY OF DOCUMENTS AS SPECIFIED IF PRESENTED AT THIS OFFICE ON OR BEFORE THE EXPIRY DATE INDICATED ABOVE. THIS LETTER IS SOLELY AN ADVICE OF CREDIT OPENED BY THE ABOVE-MENTIONED ISSUING BANK AND CONVEYS NO ENGAGEMENT BY US.

| UNCONFIRMED |
| LETTER OF CREDIT |

SPECIMEN
AUTHORIZED SIGNATURE

FORM 24300F 5/84

This exhibit is fictitious and is provided only as an example. The information contained therein reflects the terms and conditions of the Uniform Customs and Practice per International Chamber of Commerce publication #400 in effect as of October 1984.   23

depending on the commitment it has made to you.) If you have an unconfirmed letter of credit, payment to you depends on the overseas bank being able to meet its obligation to your bank.

It is important that you talk to your international banker before finalizing the deal with your customer. Your banker can give you a sense of what constitutes a normal and practical arrangement, putting you in a better position to negotiate effectively with your customer. Note that there are expiration dates on the letters as well as a shipping deadline on one of them. Once you receive the letter, it's a good idea to get the transaction underway as quickly as possible.

If something comes up that makes it impossible to perform as originally planned—a war, an embargo, a dock strike, a strike affecting you or one of your suppliers, or financial difficulties for you or one of your suppliers—it is possible to amend the terms and conditions in the letter. But that requires the consent of all parties concerned. The U.S. bank normally agrees if the foreign bank accepts the change, and that bank usually agrees if the buyer, your customer, agrees. However, obtaining agreement to changes can be a time-consuming and detail-riddled process.

Most letters of credit are irrevocable. Revocable letters of credit are not frequently used and are really little more than a means of arranging for payment; you, the exporter, have no protection prior to payment and the letter may be amended or cancelled without your permission.

Drawing the letter in dollars eliminates your foreign exchange risk. Your customer is probably also getting paid in the domestic currency, too, not in dollars, which eliminates the foreign currency exchange risk for the buyer as well—leaving the banks in the middle, adjusting their positions in either currency in accordance with what they think the market is suggesting they ought to do.

The confirmed letter of credit also eliminates your country risk. Whatever occurs in your buyer's country or economy, you are guaranteed payment. Without such confirmation, if there is a change in government, you're protected only if the foreign bank is not subject to any restrictions or currency controls that prevent it from making payment.

What makes letters of credit work is that two or more banks known directly or indirectly to each other step into the transaction and put their credit, instead of that of the participants, on the line. Even though the foreign bank may not have been willing to share the details of your customer's financial condition with you, it is willing to guarantee payment to your bank and, through it, to you.

Rules for International Letters of Credit

The International Chamber of Commerce is the rule-making organization for international letters of credit. The ICC's Uniform Customs and Practice on Documentary Credits (UCP) originally drafted in

1933, has been revised several times, most recently in 1993. Written into nearly every documentary letter of credit, the UCP rules are accepted throughout the world.

The UCP rules outline documentation requirements for all aspects of international trade, including: ocean bills of lading, commercial invoices, insurance certificates, inspection certificates, precise name and address of the beneficiary, references to mode of transport, and dozens of other conditions pertaining to shipment of goods internationally. Copies of the UCP rules for letters of credit can be obtained from ICC offices in New York City and Paris.

Variations on the Basic Letter of Credit.

There are a number of variations on the basic letter of credit. A transferable letter of credit can be used when you are acting as middleman and therefore need to be able to transfer all or part of your rights under the letter to one or more of your suppliers. Similarly, you can arrange a letter of credit that provides for an assignment of the proceeds. Such a letter does not transfer responsibility for performing; it merely shifts the assignment of proceeds.

"Back-to-back" letters of credit may also be useful to you if you are a middleman. In such cases, a second letter of credit is issued to one of your suppliers and names the supplier as the beneficiary. The first letter of credit, naming you as beneficiary, is used as collateral for the issuance of the second letter of credit. Banks are reluctant to get involved with back-to-back credits, primarily because the bank in the middle can get stuck paying your supplier if you are unable to perform under the initial letter of credit, thereby eliminating the source of payment for the bank in the middle.

A "red clause" credit provides financing for you by allowing the advising or confirming bank to make a cash advance to you, the beneficiary of the credit. Later, when payment is to be made under the credit, the amount of the money advanced plus the interest due is deducted from the total payment to you.

A revolving letter of credit is useful if you and your customer are dealing with each other over a period of time and if there are repeated transactions. You are authorized to draw up to a certain amount under the credit; this amount is replenished either when the goods arrive; at the end of a period of time, such as each month or quarter; after a certain number of shipments; or at any other time on which you and your customer agree.

A deferred payment letter of credit can be used in the event your customer abroad asks you to provide financing for a period longer than six months. In such an arrangement, you sign over the documents after shipping and receive in exchange a promise by the bank to pay you at some time after six months. Although you have a bank's commitment to pay, you are, of course, incurring interest expense, and the pricing on your sale ought to reflect that.

Standby Letters of Credit

A standby letter of credit is a letter from a bank to a beneficiary promising that if certain things happen (or don't happen), the bank will pay a specified sum to the beneficiary. Similar to documentary letters of credit, standby letters are a protection against nonperformance of obligations under a contract. Standby letters, also called guaranty letters, are widely used in international banking. In view of their growing popularity in international trade, uniform rules governing standby letters of credit were issued in 1998 by the Institute of International Banking Law and Practice and approved by the International Chamber of Commerce's Banking Commission. The International Standby Practices, known informally as ISP98, are applicable in all standby letters of credit, including performance letters, financial letters, and direct-pay standby letters of credit. Copies of ISP98, implementing the rules for standby letters, can be obtained from the International Chamber of Commerce offices in New York City or Paris.

Other Payment Instruments

Authority to Purchase. An authority to purchase designates a bank in the United States through which you may negotiate drafts drawn on your customer or your customer's bank when you attach the necessary documents. Authorities to purchase can be revocable or irrevocable; if they're irrevocable, they can be confirmed. They can also be arranged so that when you draw the draft on your bank you give it or deny it the right to demand payment from you if it does not receive payment from your customer or your customer's bank.

Cash Deposit in Advance of Shipment. This instrument works much the same as C.O.D. It's not used very often, but it's a must if you are seriously concerned about the likelihood of getting paid.

Open Account. An open account arrangement (you ship goods without receiving payment or a written promise to pay and without retaining title to those goods) is useful if you and your customer have had a longstanding and good relationship or if the buyer is a branch or a subsidiary of your company. One of you must assume the foreign currency exchange risk, depending on which currency you use for payment, and you also face country risk. (Some countries with a shortage of dollars have in the past given preference to those of their importers who needed dollars to settle payments against documents over those making payments on open account.)

Another potential complication is that if your transaction ends in litigation, you may not only have to deal with the laws of another country but have only a dishonored open account to present instead of a formal document, such as a draft that has been drawn and dishonored.

SERVICES FOR IMPORTERS
Letters of Credit

Nearly everything said about letters of credit for exporters applies for importers in the reverse. You're the one who has to pay immediately when a sight draft, along with supporting documents, is presented for payment. You're the one who has to accept a time draft (thereby creating a trade acceptance) if you don't have the money to pay as soon as the documents are received.

You're also the one who has to arrange with your bank, or with its correspondent, for a letter of credit if that's the way you and your supplier have worked things out. Almost all import letters of credit are irrevocable letters of credit, which means that the bank is putting itself in your stead in the transaction and therefore is going to look to you for payment upon presentation of the draft. Your financial health will have a lot to do with whether you can get that all arranged on an unsecured basis or whether you will have to secure, fully or partially, the bank in return for its issuing the letter of credit.

The obligation of the banks extends only to the documents being processed, not the underlying goods. If the documents refer to a shipment of bricks, but when the boxes or crates are opened you find only feathers, the bank is not at risk. The bank does not, and cannot, verify the contents of the underlying shipments. This points up a very basic rule: be sure you know who you're dealing with. Prosecuting someone who has deceived you, or unraveling a case of misunderstanding, is a lot more difficult when it involves countries rather than states.

Foreign Drafts and Remittances

Most regional and money-center banks will sell you foreign drafts which you can then mail directly to your supplier, who will present the draft to an overseas bank for payment. You can also arrange to pay your supplier by the use of a foreign remittance. To do this, you must ask your own bank to instruct a foreign bank to make payment to your supplier, adding whatever instructions or documentary requirements are appropriate.

Trust Receipts

You may find that you need the underlying goods in a transaction so that you can sell or process them in order to be able to make payment at the end of the 30, 60, 90 or other number of days provided for in the time draft. In such cases, the documents you need will be released to you so that you can obtain actual possession of the goods, and you will be asked to sign a trust receipt, which enables the bank to retain the title to the goods while you have them. You agree to hold the goods available to the bank, and you also agree that you will pay the bank the proceeds from the sale of the goods as soon as they are sold. The arrangement is in effect a loan against inventory with an understanding that as soon as that inventory is sold, the bank will be paid.

BANKER'S ACCEPTANCES

The banker's acceptance is an instrument that can be created from letter of credit transactions or that can arise independently. Suppose, for example, that an importer receives goods under a sight letter of credit and therefore must pay the supplier as soon as the documents are presented. Since the buyer hasn't had enough time to turn the goods around and generate the necessary cash, the buyer, if the necessary arrangements with the bank have been made, draws a draft on the bank agreeing to pay a certain amount at some date less than six months hence. The bank knows the buyer's credit situation and determines that the company is good for that amount of money at that time; it therefore "accepts" the draft by stamping the word "accepted" on it. Because there is an active market for banker's acceptances, the bank, as soon as it accepts the draft, is in a position to sell the acceptance and can do so easily because its credit is sound and well-known in the marketplace. At maturity, the buyer of the acceptance is paid by the bank, and the bank looks to the customer to get paid, thereby liquidating the entire transaction.

A by-product of this arrangement is something called "eligibility." This refers to the willingness of the Federal Reserve Bank to take such paper as collateral from any banks wishing to borrow from the Fed. Banks are not allowed to borrow from the Fed except on a secured basis, and eligible banker's acceptances fill the bill for collateral very nicely.

INTERNATIONAL PAYMENTS

International payments are typically processed in one of two ways: a book transfer from buyer to seller, when buyer and seller have accounts at the same bank, or through SWIFT (Society for Worldwide Interbank Financial Telecommunication), when buyer and seller have different banks. SWIFT is not a funds-transfer system like FedWire but an international messaging system linking the world's major correspondent banks. SWIFT provides a mechanism for exchanging instructions on international transfers of funds, securities, and foreign exchange for execution on a specific future date. Payments are executed by deducting funds from a local currency account and crediting the recipient's account according to SWIFT instructions.

Established in 1974 as a cooperative of international banks, SWIFT has extended associate membership (nonvoting) to major corporations and securities firms. The SWIFT world headquarters is located in Brussels, Belgium. Businesses use SWIFT to move funds to or from overseas subsidiaries and trading partners.

CHAPTER PERSPECTIVE

Doing business on an international basis represents a major source of growth and opportunity for many companies today. There are distinct differences between domestic and international business, many of which show up in financial transactions. If you or your company is new to international trade, it will take a considerable effort on your part to prepare properly for the new world you're entering. You should select carefully a banker who is well-equipped and eager to help you meet the people you need to know, as well as teach you the ins and outs of the financial side of international trade. You need to decide whether you will assume foreign currency exchange risk and country risk. You also need to guard against the risks and the problems of doing business at great distances in lands in which the law and the traditions can be quite different from what you are accustomed to. All in all, international business, done properly, can be a most challenging and rewarding endeavor.

Presenting Your Loan Request

INTRODUCTION AND MAIN POINTS

This chapter provides some suggestions for the right way to present your loan requests.

After studying material in this chapter:
- You'll know how to sell your need for money as an opportunity for the bank to fulfill its need for a profitable loan.
- You'll understand the elements of business loan proposals.
- You'll learn why projections are important.
- You'll understand why a commercial loan customer may receive better terms on a personal installment loan than those that are available to a regular consumer loan customer.

A LOAN REQUEST IS A SALE

If you are an effective salesperson, you will instinctively do many of the things you ought to do when asking your banker for a loan. If you don't treat your request for a loan as something akin to making a sale, you increase the chances of getting turned down or coming away with less money, a higher rate, or poorer terms.

Selling, in the best sense of the word, is helping people discover that your product or service fulfills a need they already have. Your product, in the case of your loan request, is a profitable loan—a flow of one or more payments, monthly, quarterly, or annually, that will produce a profit for the banker. And that's it. Your entire discussion is designed to convince your bank that it can make a profit on its loan to your company.

Start with the Overall Picture

Begin your meeting by giving your banker a simple but comprehensive picture of your request. Begin by telling your banker that you need funds to accomplish a particular purpose and that you hope to pay it back in a stipulated period of time, substituting the specifics. Tell the banker briefly what you're going to describe in detail later. Once you've done that, it's up to you to determine which of the many details you want to cover you're going to start with; what's important is to convey with conviction what your business needs are, why you need the loan, and—especially—how you plan to repay the loan and when.

Visualize your summary as a wall on which your banker is going to place hooks on which to hang various bits and pieces of information. Once you've established the wall, your banker has a place to store the details you're going to provide. Without that wall, your banker will be forced to put everything into temporary storage, then sort things out later once you make clear just what you're getting at.

The Business Loan Proposal

Generally, every loan proposal must state the purpose of the loan and how you intend to repay the loan. While specific requirements of the loan package will vary from one lender to the next, the loan proposal in nearly every case has information about the borrower, including biographies of company officers, a company history, and pro forma financial statements showing how the additional funds from a bank loan would improve your financial position. The complexity of the loan proposal varies according to the size of the loan request; a $50,000 loan for purchase of equipment requires far less information than a $1 million revolving line of credit. In growing businesses, borrowed funds typically earn more than they cost, so your banker will want to see how the additional funding from a loan will positively impact your income statement and balance sheet.

Key elements of the loan package for business loans of $50,000 to $250,000 typically include the following:

■ Cover letter stating the loan amount requested and purpose of the loan

■ Company contact information

■ Description of borrower and company history

■ Biographies of company principals (listing expertise and qualifications of each)

■ Exhibits: (supporting documents)

    ■ accountant-prepared financial statements for the previous three years

    ■ business tax returns for the previous three years

    ■ personal financial statements (assets owned and liabilities owed) and most recent personal income tax return

    ■ accounts receivable aging schedule if the financing is a line of credit

    ■ invoice for purchase price if the loan is for equipment acquisition

Presenting Your Financials

If you've got updated financials or projections, it's important to send them ahead of time, along with a brief outline of what your upcoming visit is going to be about. All too often, entrepreneurs aren't willing to entrust new financials or projections to bankers unless they are present to explain them. Part of the purpose of the face-to-face meeting is to generate an informative discussion, but that process is diminished if part of the time has to be devoted to familiarizing the banker with revised or new financials. It's going to speed things along if you can open your discussion with the knowledge that your banker is fully familiar with your financial situation.

If you haven't sent your financials ahead of time, resist the temptation to begin by laying them down on the table. Handing out any kind of papers early in the discussion can create a distraction and shift your banker's attention from your presentation to the figures on the sheets.

Brochures, Plant Tours, etc.

If you have brochures, picture drawings, or anything else that will help your banker visualize what it is you're undertaking, so much the better. The loan officer isn't likely to pass them around to the loan committee, but even so, anything that will help your banker understand your business is important in getting the approvals you need.

A loan request often provides an occasion to invite your loan officer out to the plant, either so you can demonstrate what you've got in mind or to bring the banker up to date on what you've done since the last visit. Most loan officers enjoy plant tours, and a visit to the plant or office can do wonders to help bring to life the credit file or your loan officer's presentation to the loan committee.

Bring Along Some Help

If you're not a good speaker, your accountant or another knowledgeable person can make your presentation for you or help you with part of it. Far from detracting from your request, such assistance can lend depth to your banker's perception of how your business works and what kind of people you have working with you. Even if you do most of the talking, the banker at some time is likely to direct questions at your associate. It's a good way for your banker to confirm some of the information you've provided, and that's good for you, too.

PERSONAL LOANS

Just about everything we've said about commercial loans also applies to requests for personal loans, except that personal loans are generally easier to evaluate and therefore don't require the planning and analysis that commercial loans do.

If you are already a commercial loan customer at the bank, don't drop in on the personal loan department without first asking your commercial loan officer about your request. Depending on the amount and purpose of your loan, the bank may make the loan in the commercial loan area instead, perhaps on a 90-day note basis instead of an installment-loan basis, giving you a lot more flexibility and, perhaps, a rate lower than the prevailing rate on installment loans. In that case, you and the bank must work out what reductions, if any, you are expected to make at the end of each 90-day period.

On the other hand, if you don't mind the installment loan approach or if you prefer, ask your commercial loan officer to introduce you, in person or by telephone, to the consumer loan officer who will handle your loan. You may wind up with a rate a bit better than the usual installment loan rate, although installment loan rates tend to be pretty cut and dried within most banks.

CHAPTER PERSPECTIVE

It's important to remember that your loan request is really a lot like a sales session: you're selling the banker a chance to make a profit. And that's what your meeting is really all about. Organize your discussion, have a game plan, and present the overall picture first, so that the banker can fit in all the supporting detail later. You both want the same thing—a good loan—which makes your meeting an opportunity for you both to agree on just how good your loan will be.

How Do You Look to Your Banker?

INTRODUCTION AND MAIN POINTS

This chapter discusses how the way you present your financial story influences the image you leave with your banker.

After studying the material in this chapter:

■ You'll understand how your financial statements influence the way you communicate with your banker.

■ You'll understand the way that some of the people you hire provide clues as to your professionalism in business.

■ You'll see what kind of signals your personal behavior sends to your banker.

■ You'll discover some things you can do to help your banker feel more secure about you, your company, and the bank's loans to your company.

PROFESSIONALISM
Financial Statements and Accountants

One of the first opportunities you have to make an impression on your banker occurs when you submit your financial statements. How do they look? How complete are they? Do they convey a good image of your company, or do they suggest that the financial end of things is of secondary interest to you? Statements that are poorly prepared and/or incomplete do little to assure the banker that the company is in capable hands.

If you're just starting a business, you need to find an accountant who will work with you on a regular basis, not one who merely prepares financial statements for you once in a while. He should be willing and able to educate you rapidly about finances. Inevitably, this brings up the question of whether or not you ought to hire a public accountant or a CPA (Certified Public Accountant). CPAs must be college graduates, must pass a five-part test before they can practice, and are further required to take continuing education courses in order to remain current on what's going on in the industry. Public accountants are not subject to any of those requirements and in some states don't even need a license to practice. While there are some good public accountants in active practice, you're likely to find better qualified people among the ranks of the CPAs. Hiring a CPA may also mean that the fees you'll pay will be somewhat higher, but skimping in this area is definitely out of order. Hiring a good accounting firm will likely be one of the best business investments you'll ever make.

If you need another reason for hiring a good accountant, realize that most bankers have a strong preference for CPAs as well. Bankers work closely with accountants and rely on them for assurance that the financials they are looking at are reliable. If you're not using a CPA, you're making it a little more difficult for your banker to develop the level of confidence in you and your company that you need in order to get the best financing you can.

You might even ask your banker to recommend an accountant for you. Bankers don't do that normally, but they will provide you with a list of several accountants with whom they've had good experience. Bankers and accountants not only work closely with each other on many customer relationships but are also good new business sources for each other; there's no reason why you shouldn't capitalize on that if you can.

There are three different kinds of financial statements you can submit to your banker: audited, review, and compilation. As a general rule, the more comprehensive your statement, the better your banker will like it.

An audited statement provides to the banker the highest level of assurance that all is as suggested by the financial statements. That's not a guarantee, as many have learned to their great dismay, but it does mean that company data have been confirmed with outside parties, that the accountant has tested internal systems, traced transactions to invoices and payments, and counted inventories. Those procedures do not guarantee the absence of fraud or embezzlement, but they do reduce their odds and lend assurance to the banker, and to any other third parties viewing your statements, that the picture presented is reasonably accurate and that it is in accord with generally accepted accounting principles. The latter is particularly important to the banker, who knows the conventions with which data have been gathered and presented.

Less satisfactory to the banker, and less costly for you, is a review statement. You provide the information to the accountant who in turn prepares that information in conventional format. The accounting firm does not do any testing, though it may do some consulting and make suggestions to help produce a better result. What you get from the CPA is a "does it make sense?" analysis and little more.

Least satisfactory to the banker, and least costly for your company, is the compilation statement. The CPA compiles information provided by you into conventional financial statement format but offers no assurance that the final statement has been prepared in accordance with generally accepted accounting principles.

The smaller and the simpler the business, the less need there is for an audited statement. The absence of inventories, for example, can make statement preparation and accuracy much easier and therefore more acceptable even without the audit. But if the company needs loans that are large for a business of its size, it becomes important to test and confirm the rest of the assets on the balance sheet. Collateralization can provide a way around that, but it too has its shortcomings and can add to the overall cost of borrowing, perhaps offsetting the savings realized by forgoing a full audit.

Many banks will not make loans of $100,000 or more unless they receive audited figures on the borrower. Collateralizing your loans may get you around that limitation for a while, but that can be a costly alternative. At any rate, if you're growing and likely to encounter the requirement for audited financials in the years ahead, it's not a bad idea to anticipate the requirement by several years. For one thing, when you finally do have the audit done, you're likely to encounter some unexpected adjustments to your financial statements, some of which could impact negatively on your borrowing ability; in addition, it can take more than a year to get converted to a fully audited basis, so you'll have to start the process before the current year ends. Even then, you're likely to wind up with a footnote on your statement to the effect that only this year's statement is prepared on a basis consistent with generally accepted accounting principles, and it is therefore not readily comparable to your statement for the prior year.

No matter what kind of statements you prepare and submit to your banker, you might try supplementing them with a schedule of ratios or key figures that you use for your own personal analysis of the company. Many of them may be similar to what the banker uses, but some may offer additional insight because of your closeness to the business and the industry. Your banker should be interested in learning about these, and it represents an opportunity for you to add to your loan officer's education and understanding of what your company is all about.

Projections

Most bankers enjoy looking at projections. They're interesting, and far more important, they're a sign that you're not only on top of things but are looking ahead as well. The one thing you know for certain about projections is that they will be wrong. If that discourages you, then you're missing the real value of almost any projection—the thought and research and effort that go into its preparation. Projections are a mark of someone who is making things happen rather than reacting to what happens.

Your banker will want to see actual and projected cash-flow statements. You should prepare a cash-flow statement every month, recording the previous month's activity and estimates for the coming month. (For more about cash-flow statements see Chapter 6, Cash Management.)

Business owners understand the importance of cash flow intuitively, even if they don't know exactly how to calculate their monthly cash flow. The essential point about cash flow is that it is different from profit (earnings) and for a growing business, much more important. It is possible for a growing business to have plenty of sales to customers, but the business could be floundering if customers aren't paying their orders in a timely manner. Your banker will want to know what your cash flow looks like, because the cash-flow statement will reveal whether your business is generating enough cash to repay a bank loan. The cash-flow statement is a very simple, and extremely important, business-planning tool. In essence, the cash-flow statement is a record of cash available at different points in time. You start by listing cash on hand, your bank account balance, at the beginning of the month. Then you add the cash receipts from customer payments, plus income generated from other sources, such as royalties, commissions, or bank interest earned.

Some bankers will have someone within the bank prepare projections for you if you provide the necessary information; bankers typically have one or more spreadsheet programs that enable them to do the job for you quite easily. If you prefer, you might ask your accountant to help you. Better yet, you should do it yourself; you or your computer expert can do wonders with any of the standard spreadsheet software now available.

The value of any projection is that it provides help in evaluating problems and opportunities; the value of the spreadsheet software is that it makes it so easy for you to "what if" on a grand scale. You can try as many different scenarios as you wish and make them as broad or as detailed as you want. It's helpful to build in as many ratios as you can think of and then watch them change as you alter underlying assumptions. You ought to pay particular attention to what happens to the components of working capital and the additional investments that may be needed as your company expands (or shrinks if that's one of the scenarios you're running). Overall, the entire exercise is much like sending out radar or sonar signals to determine what lies ahead—you may decide to continue on course or make major course corrections.

It's a good idea to share some of the projections with your banker after explaining the assumptions used to make the projections. Don't worry about the projections not being correct one year from now. Most bankers have had plenty of experience with budgeting and planning and know how frail projections can be. Still, few other things provide such convincing evidence to your banker that you're really on top of things.

Other Signs of Professionalism

Much of what we've said about the selection of accountants can also be said for choosing your attorneys. Lawyers, like bankers and accountants, have reputations, and it's well worth your while to ask around before making a selection. The most expensive isn't necessarily the best. And while you're inquiring about the skills and costs of different attorneys, be sure to ask about responsiveness; you don't want a lawyer who more often than not doesn't have time to respond to your needs promptly.

What about others you hire, such as suppliers or contractors, officers in your company and the rest of your employees? What about your co-owners, if there are any? What kind of impressions do they make? Your company, like every other, has a reputation; you want it to be favorable. Others will judge it, and you, partly by the people who represent it; make sure they're as solid and professional as you are.

COMMUNICATIONS

It is important that your banker feel that you are always totally frank and forthright about everything affecting your company. Few things shatter your banker's feeling of confidence more quickly than learning of bad news affecting your company from someone else, especially if you've had an opportunity to pass along the news yourself. Too many companies wait until the last minute, just before it's time to renew a note or a line, or, even worse, until after the renewal, to pass along negative news. Sometimes that can be unavoidable, but, if you can avoid it, you certainly should; such delays can seriously impair your relationship with your banker.

Another important part of the communications process is giving your banker plenty of time to deal with your loan requests. A loan officer usually handles quite a few banking relationships, and it can be very difficult to sort out all the details of your relationship while being confronted with a last-minute request. Sometimes last-minute loan requests are unavoidable, but every banker has some customers who never come in until the need has reached crisis proportions. Frequently, on top of that, the request comes during a "drop-in," or cold call, leaving the banker no time to prepare for your request or to refresh a stale memory.

Yet another significant aspect of communications is providing enough information at, or better yet, before your meetings. Most bankers appreciate the opportunity to review your request ahead of time. Some bankers take notes when you're visiting with them; others take none and try to remember your presentation later on. Either way, it's better for you to leave behind written documentation as a reminder of the points you wanted to make. Whatever you leave is almost sure to wind up in the bank's credit file where it will later serve as a refresher to your current loan officer or as a tutor to the next loan officer assigned to handle your relationship.

PERSONAL FACTORS

Finally, consider what kind of image you present personally. You should be an optimist if you're running your own business. But are you overly optimistic? Does your banker have to take all or most of what you say with a grain of salt, or can your statements be accepted at face value?

Chances are your banker, like most people, works harder for people he or she likes than for those he or she doesn't like. Do you make it easy or difficult for your banker to be an ardent supporter of you and your company?

Try to steer business in the direction of your loan officer. Some customers are very good at this; others don't do it at all. Guess which one is likely to get greater support during discussions at loan committees?

Review your lifestyle—your salary, perks, time off, office decor. None of these factors is really a problem for your banker as long as the company continues to do well and is able to support that kind of activity comfortably. But if the company fortunes change and you continue a lavish lifestyle, you can count on that having a cumulative negative impact upon your banker and your relationship with the bank.

CHAPTER PERSPECTIVE

Bankers respond better to people for whom they have a high professional regard and whom they feel they can trust. Every bank customer has the opportunity to create that kind of image within the bank. Good financials and a forthright relationship with your banker help; getting the right accountant is also very important, not only because tax laws and accounting rules have become so complicated but because bankers rely heavily on accountants and their work when it comes to understanding loan customers. Spending a little bit more on audited statements becomes a most worthwhile and necessary investment for most companies as they continue to grow.

How you look to your banker is the product of many things, most of which are yours to control. If you want the best financing you can get, give careful thought to just how you appear to your banker.

Picking the Right Loan Officer

INTRODUCTION AND MAIN POINTS
This chapter provides some insight into how to find the right loan officer and what you can do to make your relationship with your loan officer a good one.

After studying the material in this chapter:

■ You'll feel more comfortable about asking for the right person to be assigned to you.

■ You'll understand why it's not always bad when your current loan officer is promoted or leaves the bank.

■ You'll know some of the things you can do to better your relationship with your loan officer.

GETTING THE RIGHT PERSON
As a rule, you can choose your loan officer, but it takes some research and effort. The selection of your loan officer goes hand in hand with the selection of the bank you're going to deal with. Many small banks have only one person who handles commercial loans, so your selection of a bank will determine who your loan officer will be. A large bank may have several loan officers from which to choose. This makes the selection process more difficult but provides you with more options.

Finding the right loan officer, someone willing to take the time to work with you and get to know your business, is more important than choosing the right bank. It is important that you take time to seek out the individuals who have the authority to make decisions or who can influence the credit-approval process. It is always desirable to seek out people who have prior experience lending to businesses in your industry. Remember that lending decisions are made by people and each loan officer brings his or her own personal experiences and risk tolerances to the negotiating table. Loan officers in bigger banks often specialize by type of business or work only with companies in a geographic region, so it's important to identify the appropriate lender for your business before calling to arrange an appointment.

The Initial Contact

Don't walk into a bank cold and say you want to talk to someone about a loan. After you've decided on a bank, and after you've determined which loan officer you think you want to deal with, get a friend or acquaintance, preferably one known to the bank as a good customer, to introduce you directly or to call the person and say you'll be asking for an appointment to discuss a loan. This means you'll not be a complete stranger to the loan officer, who will already have a character reference for you and therefore won't sit through your first meeting wondering whether the discussion is a waste of time.

Working with Your Loan Officer

Once you've committed yourself to a loan officer, it's up to you to help make your banker a strong advocate for you and your company. To do this, you must educate the officer, not only about your own financial standards of conduct and responsibility, but about your business and the industry within which it operates.

It's not enough for you to tell a banker you're going to pay back the loan one way or another. The banker needs to believe that what you propose is really likely to happen and that if things don't go quite right, you'll still be able to pay back the loan. To the extent that the banker has no experience with your industry, you'll have to make up that lack, perhaps by suggesting a visit to your place of business. You might give your loan officer brochures that describe your industry and your products, or send press clippings from time to time if they're appropriate, for your credit file. Remember that a loan officer may handle fifty or a hundred or more accounts and won't remember everything about all of them; the officer will review material you provide before meeting with you or taking your loan to committee.

Another reason for providing written material for your loan officer's credit file is that the turnover rate among loan officers is high, meaning that you'll face the need to educate new loan officers over and over again. In some cases, this may be an advantage for you. For one thing, if your loan officer has been promoted, it means that there are now *two* people in the bank who know about you and your company. It also means that you are establishing an appeal system within the bank, which might come in handy someday if you wind up with a loan officer who, for whatever reason, doesn't want to give you the loan and the terms that you're asking for.

Become Acquainted with the Top Officials

It's very important that top officials in the bank—your loan officer's superior or some members of the loan committee—have more than a name and a credit file come to mind whenever there's discussion about your loans. Most officials say that their evaluation of any particular credit doesn't depend much on actually meeting the customer, but many's the loan officer who's found that, with difficult credits, the single most helpful thing to do is to be sure that the bank's higher-level officers know the customer too. If your loan officer doesn't introduce you, seek out the introduction. Then keep that contact alive in a casual way whenever possible.

The same point applies to the loan officer's peers. One or more of today's peers may become one of tomorrow's top managers; in addition, if there's a change in the loan officer line-up, you may well find yourself with one of those peers as your new loan officer, in which case the more you know about your new loan officer, the better equipped you'll be to do what's best for you.

Make Your Relationship a Quality Relationship

Remember that when the bank lends money to you, it's an act of faith. The people who approve your loans, whether they be loan officers or others in the chain of approval, are putting their judgment and their reputations on the line. Make your relationship with the bank a quality relationship—not only by meeting loan maturities as they come due and getting financial statements or other documents in on time, but by handling the account side of the relationship properly as well. Don't make overdrafts or payments against uncollected funds a way of life for you and your account; lists of overdraft and uncollected customers, as well as those of borrowers who are past due, tend to circulate widely within the bank and are standard fare on the agendas of many board meetings. That's certainly not the kind of publicity you should be generating for yourself.

It's a good idea to call ahead for appointments with banking officers. Even if you yourself enjoy unexpected visitors, a lot of other businessmen, including most bankers, don't. It'll add to the quality of those visits if your loan officer knows you're coming and has a chance to brush up on you and your company by taking a peek at your financial figures and rereading a recent write-up on your company. Although most loan officers can recall many of the details of most of their accounts, there are times when some of the details of different accounts begin to blur together, and you can help your loan officer avoid that possibility by calling ahead for your appointment.

Knowing You've Got the Right Officer

One way you know you've got the right loan officer is the ease of your relationship. If you don't rapidly develop a fairly cordial relationship and a comfortable knowledge of each other's requirements, then something's amiss and you need to correct it. The officer should be genuinely interested in your progress and your problems. One of the enjoyable things about being a loan officer is the opportunity to be a participant in other people's successes; it's also a real pleasure to be able to help a customer when the going gets tough. If you don't sense that your officer has that feeling about you and your company, it's time to find out why and perhaps to start looking for someone who will take that kind of interest in you.

Ideally, your loan officer will have quite a bit of experience. Even though businesses differ dramatically one from another, there is a rhythm and a pattern to things that runs through most companies, and an experienced loan officer is more likely to understand your company and its chances for continued success.

That extra experience helps considerably when the loan officer must deal with others within the bank. Higher officials are likely to be more lenient with experienced loan officers, even if they have doubts about the loan. An experienced loan officer is able to point out to you potential problem areas that you hadn't thought of and to have a much clearer idea of what can get through the loan committee and what can't. On the other hand, an older, more experienced loan officer may bear more scars from loans that have gone the wrong way and therefore might be more conservative than some young officers still trying to make a name for themselves.

On behalf of younger officers—the ones you're likely to wind up with if you're a very small business—they're more likely to have the drive and the energy to carry the ball effectively for you. If they're good, they've picked up a lot of experience in a relatively short time and may even have a long-term view of what your success could mean to them professionally. If times are busy, they may be more likely to work late to get your deal through this week instead of next or to fight harder trying to find a way to structure your loan so you get the money you want. What you want is a fighter working for you, not someone who's going to back off at the first sign of disapproval from superiors or from the loan committee.

When Your Loan Officer Leaves

If your loan officer leaves to go to another bank, it's not necessarily bad news. You now have an alternate source of borrowing at another bank, which gives you an excellent opportunity to ask about loan rates at the competing bank. If you have a good relationship with your current bank, the rest of the staff there won't have to be reminded of the competitive threat, and you may wind up with more favorable pricing or terms the next time you need a loan.

Be on your guard if your loan officer has left your bank because he or she made too many bad loans. Your bank is likely to initiate a thorough review of all of this loan officer's former loans, including yours. You may find yourself having to deal with a new loan officer and much tougher lending standards as well. So make it a point to establish a good relationship with your new loan officer fairly soon. Don't wait until the next note matures or until a balloon maturity comes due. It may not be the simple rollover you thought it would be and the sooner you know that, the better.

If you're already on familiar terms with the other loan officers in your bank, or your loan officer's boss, this is a perfect time to stop by and review your banking relationship. Ask who your new loan officer will be. If you get there soon enough and your bank has a pool of loan officers, chances are good that you'll be able to pick the next person you'll be dealing with, before your loans are reassigned.

Of course, your relationship will be more directly affected by a change in loan officer if your loan relationship is more complicated or requires handling by a loan officer with special skills. If that's the case, your loan may be automatically reassigned to another loan officer.

You will need to address the complicating factors as soon as possible, if there is the slightest possibility that having your loan pulled could sink your business. You may think your banking relationship is important to the bank—and it probably is—but your new loan officer may be handling 30 or 40 or more loans, including yours.

Most loan officers aspire for promotion, which means you may be working with a new loan officer every few years. You then have the job of educating your new loan officer about your business and your financial needs. That's another reason for keeping a stable of alternatives out there.

CHAPTER PERSPECTIVE

Don't suffer in silence if there are problems in your relationship with your loan officer. Either or both of you can be at fault, but you're the one who can't afford to have it happen. Banks do worry about the chemistry between their customers and their loan officers, or any of their other officers for that matter. Changing account officers, whether for loans or deposits, may not be common, but it has certainly happened before and it will certainly happen again. Talk to your officer's superior, or to one of your other contacts in the bank. You deserve a good representative within the bank. Speak up and ask for some help. It almost certainly will be forthcoming.

The Philosophy of Lending

INTRODUCTION AND MAIN POINTS

This chapter discusses the reasons banks are always looking to make new loans and their efforts to ensure repayment.

After studying the material in this chapter:

■ You'll understand why most banks want more loans than they already have and what kind of loans they're looking for.

■ You'll learn what banks consider satisfactory alternative sources of payment.

■ You'll learn what bankers think about credit risk.

■ You'll understand what your philosophy toward borrowing ought to be.

THE GOAL—MAKING LOANS

Most loan officers are always eager to make new loans. And there usually aren't enough borrowers to go around, so the bank that gets more than its pro-rata share of loans is usually the bank with the more aggressive loan officers.

It may come as a surprise to many borrowers that banks and their loan officers actually want to make new loans. That's good for you, the customer, but it also means that there's sometimes a tendency to "reach" for loans, to lend more or to lend on more generous terms, than should be the case. That in turn can lead to loans that go bad because they were too "rich" to begin with.

To a banker, the real test of the creditworthiness of a borrower is its continued ability to repay its loan; most bankers are uncomfortable with a loan that just sits there and never gets reduced. Bankers are less particular about whether a loan is reduced regularly (monthly or quarterly) or irregularly. Nonamortization of a loan is often synonymous with a loan that winds up going bad; many bankers know that nonamortization of loans was a popular concept back in the 1920s and that it later boomeranged with a vengeance.

Managing Risk

Bankers have loan customers because they offer business owners financing at a lower cost, and at terms more acceptable, than many of the available alternatives, such as issuing stock in the capital markets. By making loans, banks take on interest-rate risk and credit risk. As a rule, the higher the perceived credit risk, the higher the interest rate you're going to have to pay. When the loan is made at a fixed-interest rate, chances are you will hang on to your low fixed-rate loan as long as you can. But if rates go down, you may decide to refinance at the lower prevailing rates, even if it means going to another bank to refinance.

The other aspect of risk is credit risk, or the probability you won't repay the loan. That probability may be very low if your business is healthy, but it cannot be dismissed entirely. If your financial health is in any way uncertain, that subject will dominate your loan discussion. The bank's goal in making a loan is to increase the odds it will get back all of its money, plus a profit. What your loan officer believes is going to happen after the loan is made determines the amount, interest rate, and other terms of your loan.

Good Loan Officers and Bad Loans

Believe it or not, a loan officer ought to have a few bad loans from time to time in order to establish and preserve a record as an aggressive loan officer trying to help the bank, its customers, and its community. An officer who never has any losses is probably turning down a lot of loans that would have been just fine and making only the "cream puff" loans, in the process driving a lot of good business away from the bank and possibly from the community.

How many bad loans does a loan officer need to establish a good reputation? Not many. If there are too many losses, it won't be long before the bank's managers and directors begin to question what the loan officer is doing with the bank's assets. Generally speaking, one dollar of losses each year for every $100 of loans in a loan officer's portfolio is too many losses and will call for a lot of explaining.

Charge-off Ratios

An average of 40 or 50 cents lost for every hundred dollars of loans owned is acceptable by today's standards. Thirty years ago, however, that would have been regarded as a high percentage of loans to charge off each year; the desired level then was more like 10 cents per $100.

If those percentages sound small to you, remember that a loan officer needs a very high batting average in order to lose less than one half of one percent on loans. Much of the information a loan officer requests from customers is intended to help achieve that batting average. Thus, even if your banker is an aggressive loan officer, one who really wants to "reach" as much as possible, you must expect many questions during the preliminary discussions surrounding your loan.

Refinancing Loans

Many loans, especially those made to business, don't work out quite as planned, and often the terms of repayment need to be rearranged. This is not necessarily bad; business conditions change all the time, making it likely that before a loan can be paid in full, the company will need additional equipment or more inventory or will embark on a new sales effort, all of which require money. Adapting yesterday's loans to today's conditions or helping your company pursue altered goals is all a part of a loan officer's job.

Bankers get paid not only for bringing new loans into the bank but also for keeping existing loan business by serving the changing needs of those customers. Your banker needs you and should be receptive to requests for more money or for changes in the loan terms, provided there is a good reason for the change.

THE ALTERNATE SOURCE OF PAYMENT
The Need for Collateral

Before a loan is made, the lender is pretty much in the driver's seat (forgetting for the moment the effects of competition, which can sometimes put the borrower in the driver's seat). But once the loan has been made, the borrower has the upper hand—the company has the money, or whatever it bought with the money, while the banker has only an I.O.U. If the bank wants to assure itself of some flexibility and maneuverability if the borrower runs into financial difficulties, the loan officer must build those elements into the I.O.U. while the loan is being negotiated.

Above all, the banker needs a way for the bank to get paid if the normal method of payment doesn't work out. Frequently, the banker uses collateral as its alternate source of payment. There is an almost endless list of assets that can be used as collateral, as discussed in Chapter 15.

The Home as Collateral

Some entrepreneurs are willing to pledge their equity in the family home as collateral to a loan for their business. It's a very difficult loan request, especially if the loan is to be used to start a business.

Bankers know from long experience that starting any business, regardless of its nature, is a risky undertaking at best. The bank is uncomfortable but not because it feels that it would have an unsafe loan on its hands; the equity in the home would likely be more than enough to protect the bank. What makes the loan difficult is that the bank does not want to be put in the position of having to foreclose on the borrower's home.

The primary source of the loan repayment is expected to be the cash flow from the business; the secondary source is the sale of the house. Such loans do get made, but not until the banker becomes convinced that foreclosure won't be necessary or that the would-be borrower would, if no loan were forthcoming, sell the house anyway to raise the funds for the business venture. This provides the bank with the rationale that by making the loan it is helping to postpone, and perhaps to avoid, what would presumably be an unhappy event for the family.

Loan Guarantees

Another alternate source of payment is the guarantee—a legally binding agreement by a source other than the borrower to make good on the loan if the borrower defaults. Ideally, the guarantor should not depend on the business of the borrower for payment or cash flow. A guarantee is not exactly the same as collateral, and in many ways it's worse. Good guarantors, if they are individuals, are often good customers of the bank doing the lending; if the bank is forced to ask the guarantor to make good on the guarantee, the bank runs the risk of offending a good customer. That shouldn't be the case, but sometimes personal and corporate guarantors take offense when they're asked to put their money where their guarantee is.

MAKING COMMERCIAL LOANS

Banks make loans because it's the best way to make a good profit on the money their depositors have left with them. They could make a profit by investing the money in government bonds, but the yields would be considerably less because the interest yields on bonds are usually lower by several percentage points than those on loans. That rate differential reflects the greater risks involved with making loans, but it's the bank's hope and expectation that despite loan losses, it can still come out ahead by putting as much of its money as possible into loans.

How Much Interest Equals One Bad Loan?

It takes a lot of extra interest on a lot of loans to make up for the loss of principal on just one bad loan. For example, if you assume that a bank can earn 2 percent more on loans than it can on investments, then for every $1,000 it loses on bad loans, it needs $50,000 in good loans, all earning that extra 2 percent interest, just to break even. If the bank has $400,000 in loans, of which only $1,000 go bad (a loss ratio of .25 percent on loans, about where many banks would like to be today), then that extra 2 percent translates into $8,000 in extra interest income less $1,000 in losses, for a net improvement of 1.75 percent, short of the 2 percent expectation but better than what the bank would earn by leaving its money in bonds and fed funds. In short, for every bad loan, the bank needs 50 or more good loans of similar size and rate just to get back to a profit improvement of zero. And a profit improvement of 2 percent or so, after all expenses, including losses and overhead, call for better than 500 such loans.

Selling Loans

One of the problems with making loans is that, once made, they're not very liquid; that is, they cannot be sold quickly or easily. Banks sell their loans for two reasons: if there is a run-off in deposits or if the growth of loans in general is greater than the growth in deposits. Neither of those conditions is very likely for most banks in today's economy, but they have existed in the past and could very well happen again.

The losses recently suffered by some banks have produced another reason for selling assets: it is a way for a troubled bank to replenish capital (if the sale can be done at a profit) and reduce capital requirements by reducing the overall size of the bank. Credit card loans, car loans, and mortgage loans, for example, have been sold off to achieve these ends. Most of those sales, however, were rather complicated, and they are not the kind of thing one normally contemplates when thinking of asset liquidity.

A fourth reason for selling loans is to generate fee income and profits on the loans sold. The profits depend upon how the rates on the loans being sold compare to rates in the marketplace, and the fees come from several sources: the retention of part of the rate on the loans sold and servicing fees charged by the selling bank for continuing to handle the payments and other servicing requirements of the loans sold. The loan sales in these cases are part of the selling bank's deliberate strategy of generating more loans than it can hold in its own portfolio because it plans to sell them off as soon as they can be properly packaged. But again, the loans aren't really liquid assets because of the time and skill required to generate and sell them.

There is one other type of loan sale that takes place with some regularity among banks—the sale of commercial loan participations. Here again, since commercial loans are usually complex, commercial lending skills are required. The reasons for making such sales include retention of a small fee by the selling bank, portfolio diversification, the sale of that portion of a loan that exceeds a bank's legal or house limit, and developing desirable correspondent bank relationships.

None of these sales is easily consummated. Selling loans takes time and special skills, and the markets for such loans are fairly limited. That's illiquidity.

Lending Deposits Back to the Community

To do the best job for its community, as well as its shareholders, a bank should make as many loans as it can. But how many loans is that? The answer depends on the bank and the community in which it's located. In smaller communities, banks typically invest relatively low proportions of their assets in loans, because there just isn't enough loan demand in the community to use up all or even a major part of the deposits generated by that community.

Some banks aggravate that situation by turning down too many loans. Probably the best single way to determine whether that's the case is to look at the bank's loan losses: if those losses are nil year after year, then loan opportunities are being missed. (It's important that the results of several years be used since loan losses can and do vary widely from one year to the next.) If you can't find the figures for charge-offs on the bank's annual report (they're usually set forth in one of the footnotes to the financial statements), then use the figures for the provision for loan losses. The latter appears on the profit-and-loss statement and, over a period of several years, is a good proxy for loan charge-offs.

Low loan losses do not mean that if that bank were to become much more aggressive in its pursuit of loans, loans would rise dramatically in the community. Loan demand is primarily a by-product of the economic activity taking place in the community; the more the activity level steps up, the more people there will be who will become optimistic enough about their prospects to assume all the liabilities, including borrowing from a bank, entailed in expending an existing business venture or starting a new one.

THE IMPACT OF INTEREST-RATE LEVELS

The stereotypes about bankers suggest that bankers like high interest rates because high rates enable them to make a killing. If you're a borrower who's paying those high rates each month or quarter, it's hard not to think that the banks are really raking it in.

But interest is a two-way street for the banker. At the same time the bank is earning all that extra interest income from high rates on its loans and investments, it's also paying out more interest on its deposits. The bank's depositors are generally just as aware of the higher interest-rate levels as are the borrowers, so if the bank is to hold on to its depositors, it must increase what it pays out to them.

When Rates are Stable

The ideal interest-rate scenario for bankers is a stable situation in which rates never change. That enables them to set loan rates and deposit rates in such a way that the bank is assured of a predetermined spread between interest income and interest expense. Ideally, that spread is large enough to cover all operating and fixed expenses and to provide a fair margin of profit, pay reasonable dividends to shareholders, and leave something for contingencies and for growth. We haven't had those kind of conditions since the 1930s and early 1940s, when things were so static that the prime rate remained at one and a half percent for twelve years.

When Rates Float

The next-best rate scenario for bankers is one in which all rates float freely and in unison. In such a case, no matter how rates fluctuate, the banker is still able to maintain a constant spread and thus cover costs with certainty. This scenario, which sounds almost as good as the fixed-rate scenario, has more or less prevailed since deregulation removed interest rate ceilings on savings accounts and certificates of deposit in the 1970s. The problem has been that while rates are now generally free to move up and down, they don't always do it in unison. Most deposit maturities are for six months or less, which means that it takes only several months for a change in rates to cycle through the entire deposit structure. On the loan side, however, while there are many more variable rate loans than before, many rates still remain unchanged for years. To complicate matters further, the rates on some variable rate loans change quickly as the prime rate changes, while others, such as those for variable rate mortgage loans, are adjusted only once a year.

The problem is that forecasting what rates are going to do is as difficult for bankers as for anyone else; the result is that some banks are poised to do well if rates go down, while others are set to win if rates go up.

Bankers get hurt on some of their loans no matter which way rates move. Much the same thing happens on the deposit side, the main difference being that six months or so after a rate change, most of the deposit rates have been adjusted to reflect the new level.

The banks have tried to cope with the lack of unison in rate changes by resorting to prepayment penalties and by offering more variable-rate loans and fewer fixed-rate loans. They've also tried to lock in interest-rate spreads by committing to fixed-rate loans or investments at the same time they commit to fixed-rate deposits. They've tried various strategies, often highly complicated, all with the intention of making the best of difficult rate situations. Most banks come out all right on the average, succeeding with this strategy, failing with others, but all the time being careful not to rely on just one or two rate strategies. A few banks have failed or incurred huge losses as a result of poor rate strategies, but those cases are rare.

Banks are forever trying out new strategies, looking for new and better ways to serve existing customers as well as capture new ones. Their pricing strategies and their lending strategies vary all over the lot—and the variations can often mean opportunities for you, the borrower.

BORROWING PRUDENTLY

A loan is a tool, a way of getting from point A to point B. It's an expensive option, and as a rule a company shouldn't take out a loan unless that loan enables it to do something that earns more money than the loan costs. The merchant who borrows to buy more inventory needs to be sure that when that inventory is sold, the business will get back the purchase price and the carrying costs. If business is off, the cost of inventory plus the accrued interest on the loan can easily outstrip the profit generated.

Imagine, for example, a home builder who has just borrowed and then spent $80,000 to buy land and build a house on it. The asking price for the house is set at $100,000. Interest costs on the loan come to $1,000 a month. In the housing business, especially if houses are moving slowly, it can take a year or more to sell a house. That means the builder, who initially spent $80,000 on the house, can very easily wind up with a cost of $90,000 or more. Every passing day cuts into profits a little more.

Before taking out a loan, review your current situation carefully. Don't take the loan just because you've got a banker who's comfortable with you and your business and who will lend you virtually whatever you ask for. Too often, borrowing from the bank is the easy way to get to the next anticipated period of positive cash flow; the right way, and often the hard way, is to generate cash by applying tough internal disciplines to reduce interest expense and bring more dollars down to the bottom line.

A willing banker can get you hooked on loans. Worse yet, the discipline you fail to exercise today because your banker is so ready with the money may damage the health of your business to the point that tomorrow that same banker is no longer so willing to accommodate you. By the time that happens, you may have lost the flexibility you need to survive one or another of the many changes that are forever impacting on all businesses.

CHAPTER PERSPECTIVE

Most banks want more loans than there are loans available. That puts you in a buyer's market; if you can satisfy the banker's needs, your chances of getting a loan are pretty good. But the banker needs to know that your business is healthy and that you're in a position to repay the loan over time. Bankers would just as soon your loan is never paid off, but they feel that way only for as long as you demonstrate your continued ability to keep on paying. Remember that more and better commercial loans are the key to a commercial loan officer's rise within the organization, because loans are a better way to improve overall earnings for the bank. Make your banker's ambition work to your advantage.

The Loan Side of the Bank

INTRODUCTION AND MAIN POINTS

This chapter explains the role of loan committees and loan authorities in the loan-approval process.

After studying the material in this chapter:

■ You'll have a general understanding of how loan committees work and what you can do to help your own loan requests through the approval process.

■ You'll understand why it's not necessarily important that your loan officer have a lot of loan authority.

■ You'll be aware of the tendency toward specialization in many banks.

THE LOAN FILE

Most loan decisions in a bank are made by people who remain unseen by the borrower. Most commercial loan officers have the authority to approve loans up to a certain amount, say $100,000. Senior lending officers have a higher lending authority, perhaps $250,000, and can approve loans up to that amount. Loans above $250,000 are normally approved by a loan committee, and loans above $1 million are approved, or at least reviewed, by a committee of the board of directors.

After your loan application has been submitted, your loan officer will begin gathering information about your business and its financial condition. Bank loan officers call this process "building a file." The loan file will typically include any information about previous relationships with any of the principals in a business, including deposit activity, previous borrowing experience, publicly available data from credit reporting agencies, and any anecdotal information from previous contacts with customers, competitors, and suppliers if these individuals also have a relationship with your bank.

Because a borrower's past financial performance, including loan repayment history, is very predictive of future performance, financial analysis of information supplied by the borrower is a cornerstone of the loan evaluation. Bankers refer to this review as their "due diligence" process before approving a loan request. Your lender will calculate your ability to repay the loan by "spreading the financials," which is presenting historical and projected information for the periods covered in the loan proposal. The lender will calculate the critical performance ratios for each time period, and will compare these ratios to those of companies in the same industry. (See Chapter 17, Financial Statements: The P&L and the Ratios, for more information about ratio analysis.) Bank loan officers refer to sources such as Robert Morris Associates' *Annual Statement Studies,* or Dun & Bradstreet's *Industry Norms and Key Business Ratios* to see whether the proposed loan meets the bank's credit criteria for new business loans. RMA's *Annual Statement Studies* is compiled from data submitted by lenders across the United States and is an often-used source of information about the operating characteristics and credit risks of borrowers in various industries.

LOAN COMMITTEES

Most banks have a fairly formal committee system for dealing with loans. But the rules under which these systems operate vary widely from one bank to another. In some banks, loans have to be presented to a loan committee or a discount committee for approval. In others, loan officers are given wide authority to approve or disapprove all or most of the loans they handle. In those banks, the loan committee reviews loans after they've been made, or after the committment to make them has been given, to see that they are within bank guidelines. In either case, authority to approve may apply to the entire credit or only to certain of its terms, such as the dollar amount and the rate.

The committees themselves have a wide range of authority. Many committees have little or no authority for granting loans; the function of these committees is to weed out loan requests before the requests are seen by higher authorities. Other loan committees may have authority to grant loans up to the legal limit of the bank (15 percent of total capital).

A bank's annual report to shareholders may tell you which directors serve on loan committees. If it doesn't, you may know someone who has this information. And there's certainly nothing wrong with asking your loan officer for the names of those who serve on the loan committee. If you find that you know one or more members of the committee, let them know that your loan request is pending. They may even be willing to give you another contact or tell you how to structure your loan request more effectively. They will most likely have a feel for the kinds of businesses and the types of loans the committee feels comfortable with. But be careful how you conduct that discussion. You don't want to appear to be applying pressure; and, of course, you don't want to give your loan officer the impression that you're trying to go around him or her.

Most loan committees meet once or twice a week, and on demand when a larger than normal number of loan requests are pending. Some have only a few members; others have 10 or even 15 members. It's easy to imagine the influence that a single committee member can have on the outcome of any loan request.

Normally, decisions on loans are made by vote of the committee. The votes are almost always unanimous, even though there may be considerable dissent among committee members before the vote is taken. Occasionally, a committee member or two will cast a negative vote on a loan—just for the record, or to make a point about an aspect of the loan. In the years ahead, negative votes may increase considerably as bank examiners continue to toughen their policies and their efforts to hold directors more directly liable for their actions.

Banks vary as to the amount of detail they present to committee members and range from elaborate handouts, including balance sheets and profit-and-loss statements, cash-flow analyses and projections, to just a few written lines about the would-be borrower with a few details presented verbally by the loan officer.

Loan Officer's Role

Your loan officer knows your situation best and normally has a feel for the type of loans likely to be approved and the type of terms that will be imposed. The loan officer can be either a tiger who really goes to bat for you or little more than a presenter of information, a way of getting your name on the agenda, with the discussion taking place among the different members of the committee. But whether they're tigers or not, loan officers rarely get surprised by their loan committees. Listen carefully when your loan officer tells you how the loan should be structured and what information and collateral are needed.

Last-Minute Requests

You should arrange your loan request so that there's plenty of time for the bank to go through its own procedures, including preparation of paperwork, analysis of financials, credit checks, and so on. You should do all you can to make sure the loan is presented properly to the loan committee; waiting until the last minute can hurt your chances for approval, especially if additional information is needed.

Using Contacts

Nothing helps a loan request more than a few good words from a member of the board. Favorable comments on your character, work habits, or business acumen can make the difference between getting the loan and being turned down.

The good word doesn't have to come from a director. Praise from anyone highly regarded by the loan officer or key members of the loan committee will be helpful to you. It's important feedback that provides another cross-check to help the loan officer, and later the loan committee, assess the probability of your repaying the loan.

Getting that good word is important enough that you ought to make it a point to find out if anyone you know can contact someone in the bank on your behalf. Despite all the analysis and checking, the approval of a loan can be a very subjective matter; any factor that weighs in on your side can make the difference.

The Impact of Negative Comments

Negative comments about you or your company—comments that suggest you're unreliable or devious, for example—can be devastating, especially when yours is a marginal type of credit. Bankers get skittish about prospective customers who appear to be less than totally trustworthy and reliable. Even if your loan doesn't get turned down, the terms and conditions of the loan are likely to reflect the comments. So if you know that someone in the bank has a low opinion of you or your company, you'd be well advised to go to another bank for your loan.

Loan Authority

Some businesspeople won't deal with loan officers who don't have authority to handle loan requests on the spot. They believe that the higher the authority, the more experience the loan officer has or the better a loan officer he is.

Banks vary so much in their approach that any officer's loan authority or lack of it is not a good indicator of skill and experience. Some banks give out authority in multimillion-dollar chunks. Some even give loan officers the legal limit of the bank—15 percent of the bank's capital. On the other hand, there are many banks who are stingy with loan authority.

The theory behind giving high authority is that if the loan officers are qualified to handle large loans, and if that's what they're paid to do, then they ought to be held fully accountable for their loans. An interesting by-product of this approach is that loan officers are much more careful and conservative than they might be under a system where the real power lies with committees. So there's a price, however small, for the speedier service provided by officers with a lot of loan authority.

One of the major weaknesses of the committee approach is determining who is responsible when the loan goes bad. Did the loan officer prepare and present the loan well? Did the committee members understand what they were told? Did they ignore or not listen closely to what the loan officer was saying? Did they ask enough questions? Was enough material presented? More weak credits slide through committees than get past a qualified loan officer. In fact, your loan request may fare better in a committee than you might expect, especially if you've done some lobbying ahead of time and properly explained your request to committee members.

As a rule, the bigger the bank and the larger its pool of commercial loans, the more authority do its loan officers and loan committees have. Size spells experience. Conversely, small banks rely far more on committees to get the job done. Because they lack individuals with vast experience, they have a greater need for pooling the experience of their officers and directors. That experience tends to be more subjective and less dependent on financial analysis. Consequently, your loan request is likely to have more difficulty getting through than if it were handled by a loan officer or specialist.

But even a loan officer who can answer you on the spot will want time to review your situation, maybe update a trade check (see how current or slow you are with your creditors in the trade), or just study your financials. And since the loan officer has other customers making similar demands, and since some loan officers prefer to "sleep" on a request, you may find that you have to wait for your answer anyway. Generally speaking, it's best to try to fit your requests into the bank's normal approval process.

LOAN SPECIALISTS

Many large banks have loan specialists. For example, many have special departments in the mining or gas or petroleum industry (or they may lump them together into one energy department). They may have public utility departments, chemical departments, institutional departments (which usually deal with banks, insurance companies, finance companies, and brokers), aerospace divisions, agricultural units, electronic groups and transportation groups, as well as groups for defense contractors, shipping loans, and so on.

Even small banks have some specialization, but it is not as formalized as that found in larger banks. There aren't departments devoted to one kind of loan activity, but some of the loan officers have clusters of customers in the same line of work. So it is to your advantage to ask around and find the banker who has several more businesses like your own for customers.

A loan officer who is knowledgeable about your company and your industry is more likely to feel comfortable about loans to your company. Ask your competitors whom they bank with, and if they're satisfied with the service they're getting. If they are, you may have found the banker you're looking for.

CHAPTER PERSPECTIVE

Don't fight the system. Learn as much as you can about how it functions and then put it to work for you. And remember that, regardless of its structure, it's an information-gathering system intended to provide assurance to the bank that you have the capacity to repay the loan as planned, even if there's a change in conditions that is beyond your control. Focus your efforts on finding a bank that's an aggressive lender and then work with the system that earned them that reputation. Anything you can do to improve the quality of the information received by the decisionmakers, whether they be loan officers or loan committees, will help you get the money you want at the terms you want.

Loans and Lines of Credit

INTRODUCTION AND MAIN POINTS

This chapter provides a brief explanation of the different ways in which your company can borrow money from a bank.

After studying the material in this chapter:

▬ You'll understand the ways banks extend short-term credit, including 90-day notes, demand loans, and informal lines of credit.

▬ You'll understand what to look for in long-term loan agreements such as term loans, revolving credits, and construction loans.

▬ You'll realize the importance of understanding everything contained in any note or loan agreement before you sign it.

▬ You will understand the advantages of equipment leasing.

SHORT-TERM LENDING ARRANGEMENTS
Ninety-Day Notes

One of the most common forms of corporate borrowing is the 90-day note, which is just what its name suggests—a note that matures in 90 days. (The maturity can be 30 days, a year, or any other number of days, although 90 days is the most popular term, probably because three months is usually enough time for the borrower to pay or reduce the note or for the company and the banker to obtain a clear view of the borrower's cash flow and agree upon a repayment program.)

The sample note shown in Figure 12-1 can serve as a 90 day note or a demand note (discussed in the next section); it can be used for a secured or an unsecured loan. Some of the terms and conditions covered in the fine print are as follows:

▬ a list of the events of default, such as:

   ▬ failure to pay principal or interest

   ▬ insolvency of the borrower

   ▬ failure to keep the collateral in proper shape

   ▬ a determination by the bank that your company has suffered a material and adverse change in financial condition

FIGURE 12-1 *Sample Commercial Note*

CHARLESTON NATIONAL BANK
CHARLESTON, WEST VIRGINIA

COMMERCIAL NOTE

_____, 19___   ͻͻ $ _____

FOR VALUE RECEIVED, the undersigned, jointly and severally, promise(s) to pay to the order of Charleston National Bank ("Bank"), at any of its offices in the State of West Virginia

_____ dollars, including or together with interest at the rate set forth hereinafter, and payable on the basis set forth hereinafter.

This Note is payable:

☐ In one payment due on _____ , 19___.

☐ In _____ consecutive _____ installments of principal in the amount of $_____ each, together with interest on the unpaid principal balance, payable on the _____ day of each _____ beginning _____ 19___, and continuing until the entire indebtedness is fully paid, except that any remaining indebtedness, if not sooner paid, shall be due and payable on _____ , 19___, together with interest.

☐ In _____ consecutive _____ installments of principal and interest in the amount of $_____ each, payable on the _____ day of each _____ beginning _____ , 19___, and continuing until the entire indebtedness is fully paid, except that any remaining indebtedness, if not sooner paid, shall be due and payable on _____ , 19___, together with interest. Payments shall be applied first to accrued interest, then to principal. If the amount of any scheduled installment payment is not sufficient to fully pay accrued interest, maker agrees to pay the deficiency on demand. Maker further agrees to pay such increased installment payments as may be required to pay in full interest as it accrues.

☐ on demand with interest. ☐ quarterly ☐ monthly ☐ other _____

Interest on this Note:

☐ has been discounted by the payment of interest at the rate per annum of _____ per cent.

☐ shall accrue at a rate per annum of _____ percent, or at such other annual rate of interest as may be agreed, from time to time, by the maker(s) and the holder hereof.

☐ shall accrue at a rate per annum of _____ percent of / above (circle one) the rate established from time to time by the Bank as its "prime rate."

☐ shall accrue at a rate per annum of _____ percent of / above (circle one) _____ , as it may exist from time to time.

If the interest rate on this Note is tied to another rate, the interest rate is prospectively subject to increase or decrease without prior notice as of the date the other rate changes, and adjustments in any payment schedule will be made as necessary. If the interest rate on this Note is tied to the "prime rate" it is understood that such rate is the fluctuating rate of interest as established by Bank from time to time and evidenced by the recording thereof in such internal records as Bank may designate, which rate is one of Bank's base rates to be used by Bank's loan officers as a guide in fixing interest rates and to be used as the basis upon which effective rates of interest are calculated for those loans making reference thereto.

Payments received shall be applied first to accrued interest, then to principal. Any payment in excess of the amount of an installment then due or any partial prepayment of this Note shall be applied to installments of principal only in inverse order of maturity and shall not operate to postpone or reduce the payment of any subsequent installment.

☐ This Note is unsecured except that collateral securing other indebtedness of the maker(s) to the holder also secures this Note.

☐ This Note is secured by a deed of trust on real property described below. ☐ This Note is secured by a separate security agreement granting the Bank a security interest under Uniform Commercial Code in the property described below. ☐ As collateral security for the payment of this Note, the following property has been deposited with and is hereby pledged to the holder of this Note, and is subject to the terms and conditions appearing below and on the reverse side hereof. _____

_____ (hereinafter called "Collateral").

Collateral registered in Name of: ☐ Maker(s)   ☐ _____

Any property heretofore or hereafter pledged, hypothecated, mortgaged with or to the holder of this Note, or in which the holder of this Note is granted a security interest, for any other indebtedness of the maker(s) to the holder, shall secure this Note.

The happening of any of the following events shall constitute an event of default: (1) the failure to make when due any installment or other payment described herein, whether of principal, interest, late charges or otherwise, (2) the death, dissolution, merger, consolidation or termination of existence of any maker, guarantor, endorser or any other party to this Note (hereinafter called "Party" or collectively "the Parties"), (3) the insolvency of any Party, or the application for the appointment of a receiver or custodian of any Party or the property of any Party, or the entry of an order for relief or the filing of a petition by or against any Party under the provisions of any bankruptcy or insolvency law, or any assignment for the benefit of creditors or against any Party, (4) the entry of a judgment against any Party or the issuance or service of any attachment, levy or garnishment against any Party or the property of any Party, (5) a determination by the holder that a material adverse change in the financial condition of any Party has occurred since the date hereof; (6) failure of any Party to do all things necessary to preserve and maintain the value and collectibility of any property securing this Note, including, but not limited to, the payment of taxes and premiums on policies of insurance on the due date without benefit of the grace period; (7) the failure of any Party to perform any obligation to the holder hereunder or under the terms of any other obligation of any Party to the holder of this Note; (8) the failure to observe any covenant, condition or undertaking contained in any commitment letter, or in any security agreement or deed of trust granting a security interest in or conveyance of property to secure this Note or any other obligation of any Party to the holder of this Note.

THE COVENANTS AND CONDITIONS ON THE REVERSE SIDE HEREOF ARE EXPRESSLY MADE A PART OF THIS NOTE.

Witness the following signatures and seals.

Due _____	Social Security or Tax I.D. No.	_____ Signature of Maker (SEAL)
F.R.B. _____	Social Security or Tax I.D. No.	_____ Signature of Maker (SEAL)

Note Number: _____   **Bank:** _____

This Note is under a commitment ☐ Yes ☐ No   Interest Base: 365/365; 360/365

Address: _____

---

an acceleration clause providing that the debt under this note, upon the happening of any event of default, will become immediately due and payable

▬ a cross-collateralization clause that pledges the collateral for this particular loan to any other loans you may have at the bank

There are of course many other terms and conditions, and it is important that you read them all and discuss what you don't understand or don't like with your banker until you both reach an agreement. Any good loan officer ought to be able to explain the entire note to you point by point. Although the note can be tailored to your particular situation, that does not mean that the entire note can be revised. Most banks will amend the legal and financial aspects of their notes to some degree, though they would vastly prefer not to change a single word.

The interest rate on a 90-day note is normally fixed at prime or at some increment above prime, the increment varying from a quarter to 2, 3, or even 4 percent. Prime is usually the lowest rate offered by a bank on short-term notes and on most commercial loans, although there are limited occasions when subprime rates are used. The rate on the note can be fixed for the life of the note or it can fluctuate as the national prime rate changes; if it fluctuates, it can change on the same day that the national prime rate changes or at the next month-end, quarter-end, or any other date. Many smaller banks define their prime rate as that of another bank; for example, some banks establish their prime rate as that set by the Chase Bank, or that of the Chase Bank plus one half percent or one percent.

Interest is normally payable at maturity, though many different arrangements, including payment each month or quarter, can be established. A borrower who has several notes outstanding at one time may arrange for the interest on all of them to be payable monthly, quarterly, or at maturity.

At the end of 90 days, you may need to renew your note. Renewal usually entails paying the interest on the old note and signing a new one. Visiting the bank for a renewal can be the occasion for another discussion with your banker about your overall credit situation if there have been recent changes in it.

The source of repayment on 90-day notes often has a seasonal aspect to it, such as the liquidation of inventory or the payment of receivables. Other sources of payment might be one-time events, such as the completion of a construction project, the conclusion of a contract, or the sale of a particularly large item. Retailers with big Christmas seasons or contractors with busy summer seasons are good examples of companies that regularly use 90-day notes in order to finance seasonal bulges in their businesses.

Demand Loans

Demand loans are so-named because they are payable on demand; that is, by the terms of the note, the bank has the right to call upon you for payment in full at any time. The demand note, coupled with related documents, gives the bank the right to sell the collateral without further discussion with or authority from the borrower. Such notes are often used when the loan is secured by stocks, a form of collateral whose value can disappear quickly, making it necessary for the bank also to move quickly in order to protect itself.

There have been many occasions when the market dropped and the bank failed to sell before the loan went "under water," that is, before the value of the collateral dropped below the amount of the loan.

Despite that kind of history, demand loans are still popular today. They are a handy way of dealing with well-secured loans, as well as unsecured loans backed by solid credit where there's no pressure to establish a loan reduction program or get the loan paid off. The source of payment on such loans is either the sale of the underlying collateral or the financial statement of the borrower, providing the latter shows available assets that could be liquidated by the borrower if necessary to pay off the loan.

Rates on demand loans can be fixed or floating, much the same as for ninety-day notes. Typically, the interest is billed by the bank on a monthly or quarterly basis since there isn't really any maturity date at which to pay interest.

Lines of Credit

Most banks offer secured and unsecured lines of credit. These can have a fixed or floating interest rate, and the underlying note can be a demand note or a 90-day note. Most lines, even if confirmed in writing by the bank, are informal and can be cancelled or changed unilaterally by the bank. The bank's letter of confirmation will be appropriately hedged, probably basing the line upon the last fiscal statement seen by the bank and probably also stating that loans may not be available to you under the line if there is an unusual and adverse change in your financial condition.

If you must have an absolute commitment, then you should arrange for a formal loan agreement such as a revolving credit (discussed later in this chapter). That agreement requires that the bank advance money to you provided you're not in default on any of the terms and conditions in the agreement. The bank will expect a commitment fee, and the terms and conditions of the loan will be extensive.

Informal lines of credit work well for borrowers who are in good financial health and who know that if their current bank won't lend them the money they need, other banks in town probably will. Some borrowers even arrange lines with several banks, using the additional lines of credit as assurance that if the first line falls through, others will be available. That may seem redundant, given the unconfirmed nature of such lines, but banks frequently do not agree on how good the credit of any particular company is.

Many banks also use informal lines of credit to attract new business, offering them to a carefully screened list of prospects as a way of demonstrating their faith in those companies.

Clean-ups. One of the normal requirements of an informal line of credit is an annual "clean-up"—that is, paying off all borrowings under the line for a specified period of time. The clean-up is supposed to demonstrate that the company's need for bank money is only temporary, that the capital already in the business is adequate to take care of normal financial requirements, and that the bank's help is required only at seasonal high points in inventory or receivables. Clean-ups are not normally required if borrowings under the line of credit are secured, the collateral being regarded as a form of capital already provided by the company.

The annual clean-up is deeply ingrained in banking tradition, although some banks waive it on occasion. If a borrower has lines with several banks, the banks may agree that not all the lines have to be cleaned up at the same time producing an alternating clean-up arrangement (sometimes called a Chinese clean-up).

Overdrafts and Uncollected Funds

When a bank pays checks that overdraw your account, or for which the collected funds in your account are not sufficient, it is in effect making you an unsecured loan. As a result, overdrafts and payments against uncollected funds count toward your loan limit and against your loan officer's loan authority. If you're already borrowing at or close to the maximum of your credit lines, you may discover one day that your loan officer does not have the authority to pay your overdrafts and uncollected funds.

Some banks charge interest on overdrafts and payments against uncollected funds, sometimes at a penalty rates. While banks in many foreign countries offer lines of credit for overdrafts to some of their customers, banks in this country do not. Since good management of your cash flow enables you to avoid overdrafts and uncollected, and since both are looked upon with disfavor by most banks in this country, you should make it a point to avoid this kind of borrowing.

LONG-TERM LENDING ARRANGEMENTS
Term Loans

Banks make term loans for periods of one to ten years, though three- to five-year terms are preferred. Term loans are designed to fund a major cash outlay and spread the repayment of the loan, plus interest, over a period of time roughly corresponding with the cash flow the borrower and the banker estimate will be available to service the debt. Term loans are used for large projects such as plant expansions or renovations; purchases of additional equipment such as mainframe computers, rolling stock of any kind, or machine tools; the addition of a new product line; the acquisition of other companies; or the financing of increased working capital needs resulting from increased sales or added territories.

Term loans are usually tailored to the needs and expectations of the borrower, so that no two are exactly alike. Typically, though, they include many of the following terms and conditions:

■ a standby or "take-down" period that allows time for delivery of equipment or the completion of construction before principal repayment begins and allows the company to borrow or take down the money as needed rather than all at once.

■ a final maturity by which the entire loan or some portion of it is to be paid. If there is an unpaid portion outstanding (often referred to as a balloon), the balloon should be renegotiated before the final maturity date. The initial loan agreement may or may not deal with the terms and conditions under which the balloon portion is to be refinanced; if the loan agreement is silent on that point, then new terms and conditions for the balloon have to be negotiated just as though the balloon were an entirely new loan application. Verbal understandings and discussions often count for little after the passage of many years, especially if there have been changes in loan officers or loan policies and/or changes in your company's financial health.

■ the interest rate can be set at the time the agreement is signed, at the time of the first takedown, at the end of the takedown period, or at any other point agreed on. The rate can be fixed or floating (tied to prime or anything else that moves, such as fed funds or the treasury bill). Ideally rates ought to be calculated on a 365 or 366-day basis, but some notes call for a 360-day basis instead. The 360-day basis (which divides the year into 360 days, but then assesses that rate for 365 days) costs you more money, and you should avoid it if possible.

| Annual interest on a | 365 days | 360 days |
| loan of $100,000 @ 10%: | $10,000.00 | $10,138.89 |

In addition, there may be a provision for minimum and maximum interest rates. These are called floors and ceilings, and they permit the interest rate to fluctuate within those limits. Usually, you can't have a maximum without a minimum, although if you're a good enough customer, you might be able get the bank to agree to just a maximum.

■■ commitment fees that represent the price the bank charges for making an irrevocable commitment to lend to you. Such fees are typically a half or one percent and are usually calculated against the average unused or unborrowed portion of the total commitment.

■■ monthly or quarterly payments that include both principal and interest. Principal payments can stay the same throughout the life of the loan, or they can change in accordance with anticipated cash flows. There often is an initial period during which no principal payments are required; furthermore, the agreement may be designed so that the borrower can borrow under the agreement to pay the interest that comes due during the standby period. The purpose of such arrangements is to allow the borrower time to achieve delivery or complete construction so that the company can start generating the cash flow needed to service the loan properly.

■■ a requirement that all prepayments, if they are allowed, be applied in the inverse order of maturity, which means that the amount of the prepayment will be applied to the last payments due, starting with the last one and working up to the nearer maturities. This is intended to preserve a schedule of earlier payments, and therefore cash flow, for the bank; it also avoids a period during which the borrower makes no payments at all.

■■ a prepayment penalty. Many banks, once they have gone to the trouble of designing and making a term loan, prefer to have it remain on their books for as long as things are going well for the company. Furthermore, they sometimes fund the loan by borrowing a similar amount of money with rates and maturities closely tied to those of the term loan. If the loan is prepaid, the bank may not be able to replace it with another loan and may therefore wind up with just the funding portion of the deal still intact. To discourage prepayment, therefore, banks often impose a penalty for prepaying a term loan.

■■ a requirement for collateral, depending upon the health of the company and the nature of available collateral. Whether there is to be collateral or not, the agreement may contain a "negative pledge" covenant under which the company agrees not to pledge any of its assets as collateral to a loan from anyone else. There may also be a clause calling for cross-collateralization, which means that collateral that secures other loans made by the bank to the company will also secure the term loan; conversely, collateral taken under the term loan will also secure other loans the bank may have made to the company.

■ a prohibition against borrowing from any other source. If there already are other lenders, or if others are anticipated, then specific provision will be made for them.

■ a call for representations and warranties by the borrower that the financial statements reflect a true picture of the company's health, that signing the loan agreement does not violate any other agreement, and that there's no litigation pending that has not been revealed to the bank.

■ an affirmative covenants section that lists actions you agree to take during the life of the term loan, such as continuing in essentially the same business, granting the bank access to your books, maintaining adequate insurance, and complying with all applicable laws and regulations.

■ a negative covenants section enumerating things you agree not to do, including guaranteeing or prepaying other debt, retiring capital, or changing the business or its name.

■ a financial statements section calling for the submission of financial statements on a regular basis, usually quarterly. An audited statement will normally be required on an annual basis coinciding with the company's year-end fiscal date, with company-prepared figures usually sufficing for the interim dates. There is likely to be a requirement that the financial statements be accompanied by a certificate, signed by your company's president or treasurer, stating that you are in compliance with all terms and conditions of the agreement. Other information, such as a schedule of receivables, may also be required.

■ a requirement that the company meet certain ratio tests and a number of financial minimums and maximums, based on the information presented in your financial statements. Failure to meet one or more of these requirements is possibly the most frequent cause of defaults under loan agreements. The requirements are likely to include:

   ■ minimum dollars of working capital
   ■ minimum dollars of net worth
   ■ minimum working capital ratio
   ■ maximum dollars of indebtedness
   ■ maximum dollars of lease liabilities
   ■ maximum dollars of capital expenditures

- maximum dollars of dividends
- maximum dollars of loans and advances to individuals
- maximum percentage of raises to individuals and/or groups of individuals
- maximum ratio of total debt to net worth
- maximum ratio of long term debt to net worth

- a section describing the events of default—those events whose occurrence constitutes an event of default and thereby gives the bank the right to demand immediate payment of the entire loan, to sell collateral, and to take whatever other steps it feels are necessary to protect its interests. It is desirable, if you can arrange it, that there be a provision that the bank must give you thirty days after it has notified you of the existence of a default before it can accelerate the loan. Ideally, such notice will give you time to correct whatever it was that caused the default in the first place; at the very least, it will give you time to negotiate with the bank as to what the next move might be. The balances in your accounts with the bank are likely to be included in the collateral against which the bank might move in the event of default. That right, called the right of offset, might mean that you could instantly find yourself without any operating funds. Your agreement may contain a cross-default provision, meaning that any event of default under any other loan agreement you have with the bank, or with anyone else, might also be an event of default under the term loan agreement.

All in all, it's a pretty onerous set of terms and conditions. The intent is to build into the agreement enough protection for the bank so that it can give the borrower the needed money at the outset and then leave the borrower free to operate in normal fashion without interruption during the life of the loan. The ease or toughness of the terms and conditions are largely a function of the financial health and condition of the borrower and the results of negotiations and discussions that take place before the agreement is signed. Under a well-designed agreement, defaults will not occur unless the company strays considerably from its originally intended course, suggesting that something is seriously wrong and different from the conditions that prevailed at the time the agreement was entered into.

The agreement with which you begin your discussions may be a standard form from which nonapplicable or undesirable clauses will be stricken. Or you may be presented with an agreement that appears to have been written especially for you. Don't be afraid to argue and debate over the conditions you're eventually going to have to live with. They're highly important to you and to the bank, and you both should be satisfied (or equally dissatisfied) with the end product.

Bankers do expect considerable discussion and debate on something as complex as this, so speak up and be sure you fully understand the entire agreement and its potential impact on you and your company.

Revolving Credits

Revolving credits are formal agreements that contain terms and conditions identical or very similar to those found in term loan agreements. The principal differences are an outgrowth of the repeated up-and-down pattern of borrowing typical under a revolving credit. Unlike an informal and unsecured line of credit, clean-ups are not called for; the overall level of borrowing may vary considerably under the agreement, but by and large, the borrower expects to be on the bank's books for the entire life of the agreement. For example, the borrower may use the money for working capital, or more specifically, for carrying inventory and/or receivables; as inventory comes in or is processed, the level of loans goes up, dropping as payments from customers are received. Revolving credits often have formulas prescribing the maximum amount that can be borrowed at any given time; under a $500,000 revolver, for example, the maximum might be the lower of $500,000 or the total of 40 percent of the finished inventory on hand and 80 percent of the total accounts receivable less than 60 days old.

Commitment fees are standard for revolvers and, as was the case with the standby portion of the term loan, are based on the unused portion of the maximum amount available.

Financial statements are likely to be required on a monthly rather than a quarterly basis under a revolving credit. In addition, you are likely to be required to submit monthly or weekly schedules of inventory and receivables, supplemented by updated data as of the date of any increase in the loan, so that the bank can calculate the maximum loan amount to be available under the borrowing base formula.

The life of such an agreement can range from a few months to several years; one, two or three years are the most common. You should consult both your banker and your accountant on the most desirable agreement term for you, since the amount of time remaining in the agreement at the time of your next fiscal date can have a major impact on whether your borrowings under the revolver are shown as current or noncurrent liabilities. That, in turn, can sharply increase or decrease your working capital (current assets minus current liabilities), current ratio, and some of your debt ratios (see Chapter 17). For the same reasons, it may also be important to renegotiate the revolver before less than one year remains on the existing agreement.

Banks engaged in what is called asset-based lending usually use revolving-credit agreements as well. The loans in such cases may be much "fuller" or riskier than other term loans or revolving credits and rely to a much greater degree on collateral than on overall company cash flow. As a result, asset-based lending frequently requires the company to pledge plant and equipment and any other assets it might have in addition to its inventory and receivables.

Construction Loans

Construction loans are in a sense a specific application of a revolving credit; instead of a borrowing pattern characterized by ups and down, there's usually a steady buildup of borrowed funds culminating in one large payment. The final payment of a construction loan normally comes from a long-term lender (usually not the bank) who is committed to make the loan after a number of preset requirements for the project have been met; a construction loan given by a bank is usually designed to assure that all the terms and conditions desired by the long-term lender are met. Sometimes the construction lender and the final lender are the same institution, but in most cases they are not. Only rarely will a bank make a construction loan without a "takeout" commitment from a final lender; the proper financing of something like a building requires long-term financing covering fifteen or twenty years or more, a period of time far too long for banks, with their preponderance of short-term liabilities.

Advances or loans under a construction loan agreement are not normally allowed unless the bank is satisfied that the building is going along as originally proposed. To achieve this, the bank generally includes some special requirements in addition to those normally called for in a term loan. These may include such documents as:

▬ Plans and specifications, along with an agreement not to make any changes in them without the bank's permission

▬ A copy of the contract with the general contractor, along with an agreement not to make any changes in it without permission of the bank

▬ Proof of bonding of all contractors and sub-contractors

▬ Foundation surveys

▬ Certificates of completion from the architect/engineer stating that all work has been done in conformance with plans and specifications

▬ Certificates setting forth the amount of money expended to date. The bank normally limits its advances to some percentage of that total expenditure, perhaps 90 or 95 percent. There may also be a requirement that the bank, at its option, may itself make disbursements directly to contractors or subcontractors.

▬ Certificates stating that the long-term mortgage commitment is still effective and in place

GENERAL CONSIDERATIONS
Legal and Policy Limits

A commercial bank is not permitted by law to lend any one customer more than an amount equal to 15 percent of the aggregate of the bank's net worth, plus its reserve for bad debts, plus any subordinated debt outstanding. The purpose of such regulations is to avoid overconcentrating credit with any one borrower so that if that loan turns bad, the bank's capital will not be so severely damaged that the bank is unable to continue in business.

The definition of "one customer" is quite broad and complicated. It includes all companies with the same or similar ownership, as well as all companies and persons that are economically dependent upon each other. That normally means all or most affiliated companies, as well as all or most of the principals of the affiliated companies. Bank examiners are sticky about these limits; therefore, banks are also quite particular about the total amount they lend to any one borrower.

Many banks are uncomfortable with loan concentrations to any one borrower as high as the legal limit and therefore set "house limits" that restrict loans even more. While a look at your bank's financial statement (which will show the net worth, any subordinated debt, and the loan loss reserve) and a quick calculation will tell you whether you are likely to have any legal limit problems, you'll have to ask your loan officer to learn whether your bank has any policy or house limits on its loans.

Small Business Administration Loans

The Small Business Administration provides financial assistance to qualifying small businesses, primarily through its loan guarantee program. Small business loans are made by SBA–approved private lenders and guaranteed by the SBA. Most U.S. businesses are eligible for SBA financing if they are independently owned and operated, are not dominant in their field, and can demonstrate an inability to obtain financing on reasonable terms without SBA assistance. In general, about 95 percent of U.S. businesses would qualify for some form of SBA–assisted financing, as long as they meet industry-specific guidelines relating to annual sales and number of employees.

Charitable organizations and certain other organizations are not eligible for SBA financing.

The SBA will guarantee up to 90 percent of loan value (or a maximum of $750,000), depending on the loan program and the amount of financing requested. Loan maturities can range up to 25 years, although the average guaranteed business loan has a maturity of about 8 years. The SBA's primary financing program is the 7(a) Loan Guaranty Program, which provides funding for working capital, purchase of machinery, and equipment and real estate. In addition to the 7(a) program, the SBA has a number of special loan programs, including loans for disaster assistance, international trade, pollution control, and seasonal lines of credit.

The SBA, a federal agency established in 1953, has gone to great lengths in the last several years to speed up loan approvals and improve the quality of service provided to small businesses. The SBA now works with a network of private lenders, who do much of the initial processing acting on behalf of the SBA. One measure of success is faster loan approvals; SBA–guaranteed loans can be approved in about half the time—two to four months—previously required to get an SBA loan. SBA *certified lenders* perform the initial credit analysis for SBA loans and gather loan documentation, but are not authorized to approve SBA loans. A smaller group of lenders participate in the SBA *Preferred Lender* program. SBA–preferred lenders have been given full authority to issue loans guaranteed by the SBA, so borrowers get their loans approved much faster. Another SBA innovation, the SBA LowDoc (low documentation) loan program provides even faster loan approvals for business loans under $150,000. Borrowers submit LowDoc applications through a participating SBA lender and the lender uses its regular loan approval procedures. Loans are usually approved in two to five business days.

To qualify for SBA financing, you must demonstrate an ability to repay current debts in addition to the new loan requested, have an equity stake in the business (generally, a 20 to 30 percent equity investment for a new business), and have realistic business projections and competent management. The actual amount of owner's capital needed for SBA loans varies according to company history, and is determined by the SBA and the lender. A personal guarantee is nearly always required to get an SBA loan. Typically, there are restrictions on utilization of loan proceeds. However, most small business lenders require such guarantees and limitations anyway before approving a loan.

For information about SBA loans and to get a list of certified and preferred SBA lenders, contact your local SBA office. The amounts and terms of SBA loans are subject to change, so check with your local SBA office for current program requirements.

SBA loans are eagerly sought by some banks and shunned by others. They are attractive because they have a government guarantee and because the SBA-guaranteed portion of the loans can be sold, leaving the bank with its yield on the retained portion plus a 2 percent servicing fee on the sold portion. Here's how it would work out on a $100,000 loan with a rate of prime plus 2 percent:

$10,000 retained by bank × 12 percent	=	$1,200
90,000 sold to investor × 0	=	0
2% servicing fee on sold portion	=	1,800
		$3,000

The yield is $3,000 divided by $10,000, or 30 percent (before funding costs, losses on the unguaranteed portion of the loan, and cost of time and effort necessary for proper administration of the loan).

Other banks find SBA loans unattractive because they tend to be small, are above-average in risk, and have a reputation for requiring time and effort disproportionate to the size of the loans. In addition, some banks are concerned about the value of government guarantees in the face of growing pressure on the federal government to reduce all types of outlays.

The SBA normally requires all applicants to provide balance sheets and income statements for three years of operations; for new businesses, it seeks projections of earnings and expenses for at least one year. All statements must be accompanied by appropriate narrative comments. The SBA also requires personal statements for each individual owning 20 percent or more of the company's stock.

Further, the SBA requires that assets be pledged to secure its loans or its guarantees. It usually lends 75 percent against real estate collateral, 50 percent against machinery, equipment, furniture and fixtures, and 25 percent against inventory and receivables. It regards franchise fees, cash, goodwill, leasehold improvements, and intangibles as assets with no collateral value. The SBA may also require liens on personal assets if company assets are insufficient and will insist that the principal owners and the CEO of the borrower all guarantee the loan.

SBA loans are not an easy or low-cost way to obtain financing. They represent an effort by the government to provide bootstrap financing to struggling businesses provided there's a reasonable chance that, with the help of a guarantee or a direct loan, the company might in time become a healthy and prosperous small business.

Bank examiners, who among many other things are charged with seeing that banks comply with the terms of the Community Reinvestment Act (CRA),[1] are scrutinizing the performance of banks in the area of lending to small businesses much more closely. While it's difficult to assess the overall impact of such scrutiny on bank lending practices, it's probably safe to say that at least a few banks may feel pressured into making some small-business loans they otherwise might not have made.

The Leasing Alternative

Equipment leasing avoids the large down payment often required by a bank loan, so more funds are available for other business expenses and investments. Your business cash flow determines whether leasing is a better financing option than taking out a bank loan. Before deciding whether to lease or purchase, give some consideration to the expected useful life of the equipment before it has to be replaced, maintenance and repair costs you will have to pay, and the anticipated value of the asset at the end of the lease (lease termination). The expected service life of the leased asset also determines the number of months or years you will be financing the asset. The total of lease payments is tied to the cost of the underlying asset.

There are two main types of equipment leases: closed-end operating leases and open-end capital leases. Operating leases work well when you are attempting to avoid the risk of obsolescence; in this type of lease the lessor retains an ownership interest and is responsible for equipment maintenance and repairs. Operating leases may also have a cancellation clause permitting early return of the equipment financed. Under an open-end capital lease (also called a finance lease) the lessee is responsible for paying maintenance, repairs, and taxes. Capital leases are full-payout leases, meaning the lessee makes payments equal to the full price of the leased asset and under normal circumstances the lease cannot usually be terminated early. A capital lease is treated as a loan for accounting purposes and you can claim depreciation expense against the equipment financed.

---

[1] An act intended to encourage banks into making loans to individuals or companies in the banks' marketplace that the banks might not otherwise make.

CHAPTER PERSPECTIVE

Most banks are able to meet the differing needs of companies with the variety of loans they offer. Over the years, the average length of notes has increased as a result of the growing legal complexities of operating a loan business. Even something as simple as a 90-day note has now become a complex legal agreement.

It's important that you examine any loan document closely. If things go badly for you during the life of your loan, many of the clauses and covenants in the note or loan agreement will come into play, and many of them can give you considerable difficulty. While banks are by and large very competitive in their pursuit of loans, they do seek to protect their interests wherever they can. It is most important that you look after your interests as well. Understanding the full implications of your note and your loan agreement is the only way you can do that.

Collateral, Guarantees, and Personal Statements

INTRODUCTION AND MAIN POINTS

This chapter discusses the use of collateral, guarantees, and personal statements.

After studying the material in this chapter:

■ You'll understand why bankers ask for collateral, guarantees, and personal statements.

■ You'll understand how, in different ways, collateral and other forms of security can provide added assurance to bankers that the loan will in fact pay out.

■ You'll understand some of the dangers and problems in giving collateral and guarantees.

COLLATERAL

The most common reason for a banker to ask for collateral, or any form of loan guarantee, is that such pledges can provide assurance that there is an alternate source of payout. Bankers are often accused of not being willing to lend money to someone unless that person already has it—if not in cash, then in total assets. Ideally, of course, payment will come from the borrower's cash flow. But if things go awry, the banker knows that payment can come from liquidation of the collateral if—and it can be a big if—the bank has evaluated the collateral properly and is in fact able to sell it at a price high enough to pay the loan.

Collateral comes in many forms, can be pledged by individuals, companies, or corporations, and falls into one of the following broad categories:

■ cash and cash equivalents
■ stocks and bonds
■ accounts receivable
■ real estate
■ life insurance
■ equipment
■ inventory

▪▪ paintings, jewelry, and other valuables

The list is in approximate order of liquidity; that is, the items at the top of the list are more readily saleable than those at the bottom. Generally speaking, a banker is willing to lend a higher percentage of the value of the items at the top of the list than of those at the bottom.

Loan-to-Value Ratio

Lenders usually discount the appraised, or estimated, collateral value so the loan amount is nearly always less than 100 percent of the collateral's highest market value. This relationship between the amount a bank is willing to lend and the collateral value is the loan-to-value ratio. The type of collateral offered to secure a loan determines the loan-to-value ratio. Low-value assets such as unimproved land will yield a lower ratio than improved real estate such as an owner-occupied home. Cash and marketable securities are the most desirable type collateral. Marketable securities, accounts receivable, and life insurance policies with cash value command higher loan-to-value ratios than real estate, up to 75 percent of their market value. Inventory and equipment are less desirable because they are harder to convert into cash and, in the event of a forced liquidation, often must be sold at prices well below original cost if the bank demands immediate loan repayment.

Cash and Cash Equivalents

Most banks will lend the full value of one of its own certificates of deposit used as collateral. If the certificate is from another bank, a bank might balk at the loan altogether (since many certificates of deposit are nonassignable). Others require special documentation from the issuing bank so that the lender's lien on the certificate of deposit can be perfected. If the bank of account is unknown to the lender and the amount of the certificate exceeds $100,000, you may encounter other problems. It is probably easier to go to the bank of account and borrow against the CD there.

From the bank's point of view, there is no better collateral than deposits the bank itself holds. These deposits are a known quantity and can be liquidated by the bank itself. The interest rate on a loan secured by a bank's own certificate of deposit was once required by law to be at least 1 percent above the rate on the CD itself. Deregulation removed that requirement in 1986, but most banks today still charge interest of 1 or 2 percent above the CD rate.

Stocks and Bonds

In periods of stable interest rates, bonds can be excellent collateral, because their market value remains relatively steady. In recent decades, however, interest rates have moved up and down frequently, and the market value of bonds has also changed frequently. In fact, prices of government bonds have on occasion dropped to as low as 60 percent of their face value. Most banks today lend 90 percent against market value, not face value, of a bond.

Not all bonds are equal, however. U.S. government bonds, and those of U.S. agencies as well, are known quantities and are highly liquid because they can be sold at a moment's notice.

Municipal bonds, asset-backed and mortgage-backed securities, and corporate bonds are riskier, but some are quite liquid and can be readily sold in the bond market. Many are rated by agencies like Fitch IBCA, Moody's Investor Service, and Standard & Poor's. Rating agencies start with triple-A ratings for the best issues (highest credit quality) and then award lower ratings as the quality of the bond issue declines. Fitch IBCA and Standard & Poor's may use + or – to modify some ratings. Moody's uses the numerical modifiers 1 (highest quality), 2, and 3 in the range from Aa1 through Ca3. The lower the bond rating, the less likely a bank will accept the bond as collateral.

Leading Bond Rating Services		**Rating Service**	
Highest Quality	Standard & Poor's	Moody's	Fitch IBCA
Highest quality	AAA	Aaa	AAA
High quality	AA	Aa	AA
Upper medium grade	A	A	A
Medium grade	BBB	Baa	BBB
Predominantly speculative	BB	Ba	BB
Speculative	B	B	B
Poor to default	CCC	Caa	CCC
Highest speculation	CC	Ca	CC
Lowest quality	C	C	C
In default	D		D

Many municipal bonds are unrated, and unless a bank is familiar with the finances of that particular municipality, it will not regard them as acceptable collateral. Highly leveraged corporate bonds, such as junk bonds (some of which have lost all or most of their initial value), are examples of bond issues that would be regarded by most banks as unsuitable collateral.

Stocks fluctuate in value even more than bonds, and are therefore a riskier form of collateral. Stocks are rated by S&P as follows:

A +	Highest
A	High
A −	Above average
B +	Average
B	Below average
B −	Lower
C	Lowest
D	In reorganization

Again, the lower the rating, the less attractive the stock is as collateral.

Stocks are also subject to margin requirements set by the Federal Reserve Bank that specify the maximum percentage of a stock's market value which can be used to secure a loan whose purpose is to purchase or carry stock. Margin requirements, a product of the 1929 stock-market crash, are designed to reduce stock-market speculation that is fueled by borrowing against stocks. The regulations require that banks obtain a "purpose statement" from all borrowers whose loans exceed $100,000 and are secured by stocks. The purpose statement defines what the proceeds of the loan will be used for. If the loan is greater than $100,000 and its purpose is to purchase or carry securities (making it what is known as a "purpose loan"), margin requirements limit the amount that the bank may lend against the value of the stock used as collateral.

The current margin requirement, 50 percent, has been in effect since 1983. However, there have been times when the requirement was 70 percent or more, thereby limiting loans to only 30 percent of the value of the stock collateral.

Stocks that are subject to margin requirements include most stocks traded on the major exchanges and those appearing on a list published quarterly by the Federal Reserve Bank.

When a bank makes you a loan secured by stocks or bonds, it requires that you execute a stock or bond pledge security agreement, and a hypothecation agreement (which is signed by the actual owner of the collateral if it is someone other than the borrower). The bank is authorized to sell the stocks or bonds at its own discretion without any further contact with you. Normally, of course, the bank will be in touch with you as the value declines, inquiring about more collateral or advising you of the possibility of the sale of the collateral.

Accounts Receivable

Banks normally lend from 60 to 90 percent of the face value of receivables that are not past due more than 60 days. Lenders typically value accounts receivable according to a graduated scale, with the highest value assigned to accounts aged less than 30 days from the date of billing. A lender might make a loan equal to 75 percent of the value of receivables aged 30 days, but only 60 percent for accounts aged 61 to 90 days. Delinquencies (accounts unpaid after 90 days) and creditworthiness of customers may also affect collateral value of accounts receivable. If the assignment of your receivables is done on a nonnotification basis, your customers will continue to make payment directly to you and will generally be unaware of the assignment unless they read about it in a Dun & Bradstreet or other credit report.

When, in contrast, your receivables are used as collateral on a notification basis, you must notify your customers to send their payments not to you but to the bank or to its designated lock box. As payments come in, the bank applies them immediately to your loans outstanding. If you're already up to your limit under the borrowing base formula which normally accompanies such an arrangement but you wish to borrow more money, you must bring the bank proof of new receivables created by shipments made subsequent to the last borrowing under your line. Under such an arrangement, you lose a considerable amount of day-to-day flexibility while the bank gains much better control over its collateral and is therefore less likely to lose it during any bankruptcy which might follow.

Rates for receivables financing are usually 2 or 3 percent above prime for financing on a nonnotification basis, and 3 or 4 or 5 percent over prime on a full notification basis. Those rates reflect not only the normally greater credit risks associated with such financing but also the much greater staff and paperwork burden that goes with it. In addition, there may be a separate fee of about a half or one percent of the unused portion of your receivables line.

While some people regard borrowing against accounts receivable as a last resort type of financing, especially if it's on a notification basis, it sometimes can be a useful tool. A growing company, for example, may have working capital and plant and equipment needs that are growing more rapidly than its profits. In such cases, if the company is to continue to grow, it may have no way to generate the needed cash except by borrowing against its receivables (and inventory, and anything else that's available).

For companies that have come upon hard times, receivables financing may be the difference between surviving and going bankrupt. Borrowing against the company's receivables buys time to turn things around and get back to a less loan-dependent way of operating.

Receivables financing on a notification basis requires almost daily visits to the bank, frequent reports, and a constant if not fevered attention to cash flows. It certainly does not create the best of climates for managing a company. Perhaps even more important, when a company resorts to receivables financing, it should realize that it is sharply reducing its margin for error. It is not a step to be taken lightly.

Real Estate

Real estate is not very liquid collateral, but its value can be fairly well established and can be realized if there is enough time to arrange for its sale in orderly fashion. Banks usually rely upon appraisals by independent third parties, preferably MAI (Member, Appraisal Institute) appraisers, to establish values against which they will lend. These appraisals can range from very conservative to quite optimistic, so even though banks will generally lend 75 to 85 percent against the appraisal value, the size of the actual loan can vary significantly, depending upon which appraiser is used and what approach is taken to establish value. Loan-to-value ratios for unimproved or vacant real estate are much lower, as low as 30 percent of the appraised value. Factors with the largest impact on the value of any property are the cash flow of the property itself, the values of nearby comparable property sold recently, and the specialty nature, if any, of the property.

Real estate is often thrown into a large pot of collateral and may be included with accounts receivable, inventory, and equipment to provide for overall financing for the company. The loan may be broken into separate pieces, including a line to deal with short-term fluctuations in borrowing needs and a long-term loan to meet the company's need for financing plant equipment and working capital. All the collateral is typically pledged to secure all the loans.

Rates vary considerably, depending upon the health of the borrower, the maturity of the loans, and the quality and marketability of the collateral. A standalone mortgage loan, whether fixed or floating, may bear a rate of 1 or 2 percent over prime. Fixed rates are usually higher, at least at the outset, than floating rates.

Loans secured by real estate have come under extremely close scrutiny by the bank examiners from the Office of the Comptroller of the Currency, the primary regulator for national banks. Those examiners are focusing almost exclusively on "real estate-related" loans made by the larger banks around the country, with the result that those banks, and most other banks as well are sharply altering the conditions under which they make real estate loans. More and more banks are lowering the percentages they will lend against real estate collateral, are insisting upon much stronger cash flows, and are also requiring far more data from companies and guarantors in order to support the values and cash flows said to underlie the real estate collateral.

Life Insurance

There are two reasons for securing a loan with life insurance: the cash surrender value of a policy represents a fairly liquid type of collateral and the face value of the policy provides some assurance to the bank that it will not suffer a loss should the borrower die before the loan is repaid. A problem with such collateral is that, as a rule, the amount of the cash surrender value is considerably less than a company's normal borrowing needs; therefore, using that cash surrender value as collateral can often be used only to secure small special-purpose loans.

In a sense, the assignment of a life insurance policy as collateral represents the ultimate in illiquidity, since the principal has to die in order for the bank to be paid off in full if the borrower defaults. At the same time, there have been instances where the principals of companies have asked for or suggested this kind of protection, not so much out of concern for the bank, but because of the benefits it produces for both the company and the owner's family should it wish to sell the company on the death of the owner; having been paid by the insurance company, the bank will not need to press the family to make a quick sale in order to settle its account.

Equipment

Equipment is usually highly illiquid collateral, even more so than real estate, because of its specialized nature and because it can depreciate, deteriorate, or become obsolete quite quickly. While equipment-backed loans are sometimes handled separately from the rest of a company's financing, equipment often becomes part of a collateral package that also includes real estate, receivables, and inventory. There are no standard rates for equipment loans; it's largely a matter of what you and your banker work out and what the financial condition of your company suggests. The more marketable and less specialized your equipment, the higher the amount the banker is likely to lend against it.

Many banks finance the purchase of new equipment, allowing terms of three to five years for repayment. They generally lend 80 percent or so against the cost but go up to 100 percent if all or part of the rest of the company's already-owned equipment is part of the collateral.

Inventory

Very often when a company borrows against its receivables, it is asked to pledge its inventory as well. Banks usually are willing to make an advance against inventory of 40 percent; the percentage fluctuates depending on the nature of the inventory and its saleability. If any of your suppliers are retaining liens on the inventory which they ship to you, that inventory is excluded from your borrowing base with the bank. Most banks do not expect to be able to realize much from the sale of inventory if they ever have to sell it in order to recoup on a bad loan; more often than not, the pledge of inventory will be part of an "abundance of caution" approach by the bank—that is, it is seen as offering a slight extra measure of protection. Inventory in the hands of a banker is about as illiquid as an asset can get.

As is the case with receivables financing, rates on inventory are high because of the high risk involved as well as the much greater involvement of staff and paper work. Interest rates of 3 to 5 percent over the prime rate, plus fees of one half to one percent on the unused portion of the line, are typical.

Paintings, Jewelry, and Other Valuables

Items like paintings and jewelry are proposed for collateral usually because they are owned by the principal of the company and the company has already used all or most of its assets as collateral. Appraisals can be obtained for personal items like this, but the items themselves are highly illiquid, largely because they tend to be expensive and appeal to very limited numbers of people. There are no generalizations to be made for this kind of lending, other than to say that most banks have little or no interest in such items as collateral; because of that, they lend relatively little against their asserted value.

GUARANTEES

A bank asks for a guarantee—a pledge from a source other than the borrower to repay a loan should the borrower default—for two reasons: to add financial strength by creating or enhancing the probability of an alternate payout and to provide some assurance that the principal will remain involved with the business for as long as possible.

Guarantees, whether secured or unsecured, are a way of bringing other assets into play, if necessary, so that the loan can be repaid. If the borrower is not strong enough financially to support the loan being requested, then the guarantor makes up for the deficiency by agreeing to pay the loan if it goes into default, either by making the regularly scheduled payments as they come due, by paying off the entire loan, by investing money in the borrower's company (thereby acquiring some degree of ownership) or by providing the bank with assets to secure the loan to the bank's satisfaction.

As a rule, banks prefer to receive unlimited guarantees. There are a number of variations on the limited guarantee; the guarantor may agree to provide only up to a certain amount of money instead of enough to pay off the entire loan, the guarantee may become effective only in case of a certain event, or it may provide only enough money to the borrower to maintain a predetermined level of working capital or net worth. No matter what the form, the purpose is the same—to beef up the financial strength of the borrower without calling upon the guarantor at the outset to invest the money required. The effect is that it gives time to the borrower to prove that it can in fact stand on its own without resort to outside support guarantees.

Another form of guaranty is a subordination agreement. The lender wants assurances that the bank loan will be paid before the borrower pays other creditors, employee salaries, or transfers company assets to a personal account. A loan to the business by one of its officers has a secondary claim after the bank loan.

Guarantees keep the principals of the company as involved as possible for as long as possible. Most owners of a company do this anyway, but some, as their company sinks, simply walk away and leave the creditors to divide among themselves what little can be realized from the remains of the company. If a guarantor stands behind a company, that premature departure is made a little more difficult for the principal because the guarantee converts company obligations into personal obligations, making abandonment of the company a lot less attractive alternative.

Personal and Spousal Guarantees

In the past, banks routinely asked for not only the principal's guarantee but that of the spouse as well. Today, however, under consumer protection laws, banks may no longer require a spousal guarantee. The bank can, if it finds that a credit is too weak, explain to the would-be borrower that the credit needs bolstering in one way or another, leaving it to the borrower to figure out what, if any, additional collateral or guarantees are available and might be helpful.

Guarantees, unless they are secured by collateral, usually involve submitting financial statements of the guarantor so that the bank can reasonably determine whether and how the guarantor will be able to make good on the guarantee if necessary.

Most entrepreneurs, if asked to guarantee loans, accept the idea readily and even expect to be asked to do so. Their rationale is simple: they can hardly ask the banker for money if they themselves are unwilling to stand behind the loan and commit to do everything possible to see that the loan is paid in full. Other principals, however, refuse to guarantee their loans and seem personally offended by the request. Needless to say, banks become concerned when principals of companies refuse to put their name and worth behind a loan even though they are the primary beneficiaries of the success of the company. Some bankers feel quite strongly about guarantees and refuse to lend to any company, except on a secured basis, whose principal refuses to guarantee; other banks do not insist on guarantees unless the loan exceeds some predetermined amount, such as $100,000.

Banks are reluctant to lend without a guarantee because they know that they and the borrower may face a difficult situation further down the road if the company comes on hard times. As the company's credit deteriorates, the bank will begin to push harder and harder for a guarantee and may refuse to renew the loan. It may even threaten to accelerate the loan unless it receives a guarantee. The borrower at that point must either come up with the guarantee or find another bank willing to provide financing without guarantees—which, if the credit of the company is deteriorating, may be an extremely difficult thing to do.

Drawbacks of Guarantees

Often, as a company grows, so do the size of its loans; at some point the personal assets of the guarantor are overshadowed by the size of the loans. Eventually, the principal may well ask to be released from the guarantee. At this point, the company may have become an attractive prospect to other banks who will offer to lend without a guaranty. In such cases, the banker must relent, although some banks resort to an interim remedy, a limited guarantee reducing the potential burden on the owner's personal assets while still keeping the principal financially in back of the company to a significant degree.

Some guarantors are more than willing to make good on their guarantee, although they may try, at least initially, to buy time to satisfy themselves that the borrower really can't make payments anymore. Sometimes, however, it turns out that the guarantors haven't stayed current on the borrower's finances and are surprised when they hear from the bank that the borrower is in financial difficulty. Some guarantors, who may themselves be good customers of the bank, take that news in stride, while others become angered and threaten to pull all of their business out of the bank, costing the bank a valued and profitable relationship. As a result, collecting on guarantees is not a favorite task for bankers and is one of the reasons that they are reluctant to make loans if it is likely that the banker will sooner or later be forced to call upon the guarantor for payment.

PERSONAL STATEMENTS

Your banker will ask you to prepare a personal financial statement if you are to be the borrower or if you are going to guarantee loans to someone else, to your own company, or to a company belonging to someone else. (Figure 13-1, at the end of this chapter, is a blank statement form that you should fill out or use as a guide in the preparation of your own statement.) Such statements are quite straightforward, but you may find that there is a considerable amount of work involved in digging out all the information you need to fill it out properly.

To begin with, you need to decide whether you are going to submit a joint statement with your spouse or an "alone" statement. A joint statement is appropriate if you're both going to guarantee; if only you are to be the guarantor, you need to be sure to omit jointly owned assets on the statement or to indicate how any that are listed divide between the two of you. Only your proportionate share of the value should be shown on the statement as a part of your assets.

The preferred date for most statements is December 31. However, if there are financial transactions between you and your company, the date of your statement should be the same as the fiscal date of your company so that the banker can match up the indebtedness on your statement and that of company.

Here are some simple do's and don't's to follow in the preparation of the statement:

■ Do not show assets net of liabilities that relate to them. For example, in listing your home, your estimate of its value should be among your assets, and the amount of the mortgage on it should be shown separately on the liability side. If you hold notes or other assets which you have pledged as collateral, do not show them as net either. Show the separate values.

■ Round out your entries to the nearest thousand.

FIGURE 13-1 *Sample personal financial statement*

PERSONAL FINANCIAL STATEMENT

Submitted to THE CHARLESTON NATIONAL BANK

Post Office Box 1113, Charleston, West Virginia 25324

IMPORTANT: Read these directions before completing this Statement

☐ If you are applying for individual credit in your own name and are relying on your own income, or assets and not the income or assets of another person as the basis for repayment of the credit requested, complete only Sections 1, 3 and 4.

☐ If you are applying for joint credit with another person, complete all Sections and provide information in Section 2 about the joint applicant. If appropriate, the joint applicant may complete a separate personal financial statement (C-100), and the applications may be submitted together.

☐ If you are applying for individual credit but are relying on income from alimony, child support, or separate maintenance or on the income or assets of another person as a basis for repayment of the credit requested, complete all Sections. Provide information in Section 2 about the person whose alimony, support, or maintenance payments or income or assets you are relying on. Alimony, child support, or separate maintenance income, need not be revealed if you do not wish to have it considered as a basis for repaying this obligation.

☐ If this statement relates to your guaranty of the indebtedness of other person(s), firm(s), or corporation(s), complete Sections 1, 3 and 4.

Section 1 - Individual Information (type or print)	Section 2 - Other Party Information (type or print)
Name	Name
Address	Address
City, state & zip	City, state & zip
Position or occupation	Position or occupation
Business name	Business name
Business address	Business address
City, state & zip	City, state & zip
Length of employment	Length of employment
Res phone Bus phone	Res phone Bus phone

Section 3 - Statement of Financial Condition as of _____ 19 _____

Assets (Do not include assets of doubtful value)	In dollars (omit cents)	Liabilities	In dollars (omit cents)
Cash on hand and in this bank		Notes payable to banks-see Schedule E	
Cash in other banks		Notes payable to other institutions-see Schedule E	
U S Gov't & marketable securities-see Schedule A		Due to brokers	
Non-marketable securities see Schedule B		Amounts payable to others-secured	
Securities held by broker in margin accounts		Amounts payable to others-unsecured	
Restricted control, or margin account stocks		Accounts and bills due	
Real estate equities see Schedule C		Unpaid income tax	
Accounts, loans and notes receivable		Other unpaid taxes and interest	
Automobiles		Real estate mortgages payable-see Schedules C & E	
Other personal property		Other debts (car payments, credit cards, etc.)-itemize	
Cash surrender value-life insurance-see Schedule D			
Other assets -itemize see Schedule F if applicable			
		Total Liabilities	
		Net Worth	
Total Assets		Total Liabilities and Net Worth	

Section 4 - Annual Income For Year Ended _____ 19 ___	Annual Expenditures	Contingent Liabilities			Estimated Amounts
Salary, bonuses & commissions $ _____	Mortgage/rental payments $ _____	Do you have any	Yes	No	$ _____
Dividends & interest _____	Real estate taxes & assessments _____	Contingent liabilities (as endorser co maker or guarantor?	☐	☐	_____
Real estate income _____	Taxes, federal state & local _____	On leases? on contracts?	☐	☐	_____
Other income (alimony, child support or separate maintenance income need not be revealed if you do not wish to have it considered as a basis for repaying this obligation) _____	Insurance payments _____	Involvement in pending legal actions?	☐	☐	_____
	Other contract payments loan payments charge cards etc.) _____	Other special debt or circumstances?	☐	☐	_____
	Alimony, child support, maintenance _____	Contested income tax liens?	☐	☐	_____
	Other expenses _____	If yes to any questions(s) describe			
Total $ Income	Total $ Expenditures	Total $ Contingent Liabilities			

(COMPLETE SCHEDULES AND SIGN ON REVERSE SIDE)

■■■ Do not use approximate numbers if exact ones are available. Too many zeros suggest that you're guessing at values and not taking time to develop accurate information. If the banker thinks it's not that important to you, the banker may lose interest too.

▬ Do show your contingent liabilities, such as loans you guarantee. If you're guaranteeing loans to your company, the loan figures on your statement should match the figures on the company statement. If you're involved in litigation, let your banker know about that.

▬ Do watch out for the "value of your company" trap. Be realistic, even conservative, in putting a value on the stock you hold in your company. An outrageously inflated figure calls your judgment or your honesty into question and can damage the comfort level your banker may have with you and the rest of the figures on your statement.

▬ Do not, for the same reasons, inflate the figures for the market value of your house or other real estate held or for personal belongings.

▬ Do provide income information after checking with your banker to see exactly what is needed. Many banks accept, even prefer, tax returns, which, if nothing else, will save time for you since you should already have prepared them.

In short, remember that your personal statement will speak well of you if it is clear and complete and conservative.

CHAPTER PERSPECTIVE

If a loan makes good sense, there is nothing wrong with agreeing to collateral or guarantees if that's what the banker feels is necessary to make the credit satisfactory to the bank. By borrowing more money and using collateral to support the loan, however, you are reducing your company's margin for error, something about which both you and your banker should be seriously concerned.

When you personally guarantee a loan, you are putting your family and your lifestyle at risk. That can be a perfectly appropriate risk to take, but you need to think it through carefully. The smaller your company, the more likely it is that you will be required to guarantee loans to your company.

If your company is struggling to make a go of it and is borrowing heavily, you might consider the possibility of a guarantor. If you're skimping on working capital and necessary equipment, you may be lowering your chances for success. Someone else's guarantee, despite the problems it creates for bankers and despite what it might cost you in terms of a shared ownership, may very well be worth all of that and then some.

Collateral and guarantees can be sources of valuable assistance to you and your company, but they also can carry significant price tags. Be aware.

Financial Statements: The Balance Sheet

INTRODUCTION AND MAIN POINTS

This chapter takes a look at financial statements from a banker's point of view.

After studying the material in this chapter:

■ You'll see why a banker may feel your inventory, receivables, and other assets are worth less than your balance sheet suggests.

■ You'll understand why the banker may be inclined to give full value to the liabilities on your balance sheet.

■ You'll understand why bankers feel that the net worth of a company is so important.

WHAT IS A FINANCIAL STATEMENT?

Financial statements, comprising the balance sheet and the income and expense statement, are three-dimensional pictures of how well your company has done for a certain period of time. The balance sheet provides a two-dimensional financial photograph of the company as of the date of the statement. The third dimension, the one that gives it depth, comes from the income and expense statement, which summarizes the company's performance over a period of time preceding the date of the balance sheet and helps explain changes which have taken place in the balance sheet. The latter, often referred to as a profit and loss statement or P&L, is discussed in detail in Chapter 17.

The generation and use of financial statements is one of the most important parts of the paperwork burden that goes with running a business. Many small-business owners put paperwork very low on their list of priorities. While that's understandable, it can also be disastrous. The preparation of proper financials pulls together a lot of loose ends that tend to be overlooked in normal day-to-day activity and forces a discipline and organization that can be as important to a company as checking landmarks can be to a sailor. While the sailor may always know generally where he is, it is his frequent position checks that tell him his specific location and that keep him off the reefs and shoals that would otherwise destroy his boat. Proper attention to and understanding of the financials will keep most businesses off the financial reefs and shoals as well. Even more important, they can help the business maximize its opportunities.

THE RELATIONSHIP BETWEEN THE P&L AND THE BALANCE SHEET

As its name implies, the P&L shows whether the company has had a profit or a loss for the particular period of time it covers. After expenses are subtracted from all forms of income, what's left is profit. That profit is added to the balance sheet in a section called net worth, which is just what its name implies: the net of the total value of all of the company's assets minus the total of all the company's indebtedness. While the balance sheet and the P&L are totally different kinds of statements, they are closely intertwined, and you should never try to evaluate one without also evaluating the other.

In a sense, the net worth section of the balance sheet is like a tank filled with hope. The dollar value of net worth is what the owner(s) hope they will be able to receive at some future date when the company is either liquidated or sold. Typically, if the company is liquidated or sold under distress, the tank will yield less than its gauge (the dollar value of net worth) suggests. If the company is sold as a going and successful concern, then the tank will probably yield more than the reading on the gauge. Never look at a company's net worth without pondering what the underlying values really are for all of the entries on both the balance sheet and the P&L.

Net worth is also a liability of sorts. In a liquidation of the company, the owners get paid last, if there's anything left to pay them with. On the other hand, if the company is sold, the owners get paid first, because new owners come along and substitute themselves for the original owners, thus preserving the preferential role of the company's regular creditors.

THE BALANCE SHEET

Bankers always look for an alternative way of getting paid in case things don't work out as the borrower had originally intended. Thus, when bankers look at your financial statements with their alternate-payout mindset, they look for clues that suggest how well or how poorly that alternate payout will turn out. Bankers tend to have a conservative view of the values assigned to the various assets on a balance sheet. They want to know how those values were determined because they have a keen sense of what they might not be.

Inventory

The figure used for inventory is usually the price paid for it, including, in addition to the raw material cost, the cost of whatever manufacturing or processing has been done as of the date of the financial statement. Once processed into a finished product, the inventory normally remains on the balance sheet at cost, even though at that point it can be sold under normal circumstances at a price greater than its cost.

While that sounds simple and straightforward, it really isn't. The ability to sell that finished product, thereby substantiating and even increasing the value on the balance sheet, depends on many things other than the cost of the product, including the interplay of supply and demand in the marketplace, the relative quality of the product itself, and your company's skills in marketing and servicing its products. If the company isn't effective or if it's in poor financial health, the likelihood diminishes that the inventory will be sold at a proper price; as that happens, values on the balance sheet begin to diminish. In other words, the real values of assets tend to depend on just how good the company is at what it does—something bankers must evaluate if they are to assure themselves that the values for the various assets on the company's balances sheet are accurate.

As hard as it is to assign values to finished product inventory, it's even worse for in-process inventory. The raw material you've started to modify for your own purposes has virtually no value to anyone else. Typically it can neither be restored to its original condition nor finished by someone else—which makes it worth scrap and little more.

What if your sales are down or flat when others in the industry are experiencing growth? If you, with all your connections in the industry, with all your established sales outlets, can't move that inventory, your banker would be lucky to be able to sell it, if things ever got to that point, at even half the price at which you could move it. The banker can't help wondering if it's a product whose time has come and gone or if the competition has developed a better or cheaper product—all of which gives rise to questions as to the appropriateness of the inventory values on the balance sheets.

There's an almost endless list of things and situations that affect the value of inventory. As the entrepreneur, you must have an optimistic and energetic outlook on your chances for success. At the same time, your banker will almost certainly be more pessimistic than you and therefore be likely to attach rather different "real" values to the numbers printed on your financials.

Receivables

Accounts receivable ought to be a fairly straightforward item. All too often though, there are cases in which all or a portion of that seemingly solid item on your balance sheet becomes worthless.

The problem is primarily the seller's fault. There is a strong temptation to pursue sales without properly checking out the credit of new customers or to be too generous to long-time customers whose recent credit experience has been poor. A policy of thoroughly checking your customers' credit normally pays off in a high percentage of good receivables and a dependable cash flow. But proper credit checks won't eliminate all your bad debts. You and the banks and the credit agencies and the other credit sources you use within your industry will never be able to predict accurately all the financial problems that may lie ahead for your customers. Still, thorough and consistent credit practices will reveal most potential problems. Then you can decide whether to ship at all, ship C.O.D., price your product higher for certain customers, or get collateral or personal guarantees to help assure that you will in fact get paid what you're owed.

Lax collection procedures are another reason that receivables turn out to be worth less than the value shown on the balance sheet. Most people don't like dunning others for money owed, but even so, it's important to stay on top of your accounts receivable. Your customers should know that any time they're past due, you're going to be after them.

What's going to make your banker happy when he or she looks at the accounts receivable on your statement is evidence that you're on top of those receivables. You can demonstrate that by aging your receivables (sorting them by number of days past due) and actively pursuing overdue accounts. You should also consider adopting a policy of writing down past due receivables after ninety days, or whatever period you think is appropriate; setting up a reserve on your statement for receivables that might go bad; and developing some ratios on your loss experience each year. It's a good idea to let your banker know what you're doing, either verbally or in the transmittal letter that accompanies your financials into the bank.

Such steps take extra effort. But they're worth it, since they not only help preserve the values on your balance sheet but, perhaps equally important, reduce the amount by which your banker is likely to discount those values the next time you've got a loan request in the works.

Plant and Equipment

As is the case with inventory, the components of plant and equipment may be worth an amount that differs significantly from their initial cost or from the net value at which they appear on the balance sheet.

For one thing, plant and equipment are subject to depreciation. Equipment wears out and becomes outmoded; its value to the company can change as the company alters directions and moves into new, different product lines. At the same time, other types of equipment can hold their value or even increase in value, especially if they're well maintained and regularly enhanced as new developments come along.

Buildings and property can also increase or decrease in value. Both you and your banker are likely to be aware of changing real estate values; if they're going up, you undoubtedly will point out to your banker that the business is really worth more than the figures show because the building is now worth more than the balance sheet figure of cost less depreciation, supporting your contention with examples of recent sales of comparable properties. Most specialty properties, including many commercial properties, don't really have an accurate market value until they're sold; therefore, for as long as you remain in the plant you're currently occupying, you're not going to find out what that value really is and are stuck with the figure on your balance sheet, except to the extent that you've been able to modify the perception in the mind of your banker.

The accumulated depreciation shown on the balance sheet is the accountant's way of speading the cost of a building or a piece of equipment over its estimated life rather than expensing it during the year in which it was acquired. Without depreciation, there would be significant ups and downs in company profitability which would reveal little if anything about the company's overall success.

Bankers tend to start with the value of plant as shown on the balance sheet, original cost less depreciation to date, then modify that figure in accordance with current real estate trends of which they're aware. They're more likely to write equipment down sharply in their mind because it is often so highly specialized that it is often of no real use to anyone else without considerable and costly modification. If there are unique values there in either your plant or your equipment, it's up to you to help your banker discover them.

Goodwill

Goodwill is the way an accountant books the amount by which the price you paid for something exceeded the book value (cost less depreciation, or in the case of an entire company, its net worth) for that item. Presumably, your company saw values that were not reflected on the seller's books and thus paid the price that it did. It's likely that none of the goodwill will be deductible for tax purposes, but you and your accountant may decide to depreciate the goodwill, and the rest of the assets involved in the purchase, on different timetables. The handling of goodwill can be a tricky area from an accounting point of view and is therefore something your banker is likely to discount heavily in evaluating your net worth unless you provide a reason to treat it differently. If you include goodwill on your financial statement, you should either understand its meaning and method of calculation or bring your accountant with you the first time you show the statement to your banker.

Most bankers automatically write goodwill down to zero in their minds, adding something back if there are special reasons for doing so. The primary impact of that approach is to reduce your net worth by the amount of the goodwill. In many cases, that reduction produces a major change in your net worth and has a significant negative impact on some of the ratios used by your banker in analyzing your financials.

Other Assets

Normally, cash as listed on a balance sheet represents the amount on deposit at the bank, including uncollected deposits included in the bank statement as of your statement date. Sometimes cash also includes cash equivalents such as certificates of deposit, but these really should be broken out separately. If any cash is pledged as collateral, then it too ought to be broken out and shown separately.

The final category of assets, called other assets, can show up as a current or a noncurrent asset and tends to be a dumping ground for a lot of miscellaneous items that don't fit comfortably anywhere else on the balance sheet or that aren't large enough to be of interest to anyone. If other assets is a relatively large item on your balance sheet, your banker is likely to start asking questions. It may be that some items included in this category ought to be broken out and shown separately, particularly if they carry a negative connotation. The statement should be a valuable tool in building up the banker's confidence in you and your company; you certainly don't want the banker to feel that you're trying to conceal potentially damaging information.

Liabilities

Bankers are probably guilty of a double standard when it comes to analyzing a balance sheet. While they're inclined to discount assets, they usually give full weight to all of the liabilities. They do this because they know from experience that liabilities are usually paid in full as long as enough money can be realized by the liquidation of assets. That weighting of liability values, along with the discounting of asset values, can significantly reduce your company's net worth in the banker's mind. This, in turn, can have a significant impact on how large a loan you get and on the terms and conditions which go with that loan.

Notes Payable

The category of notes payable covers a multitude of debts, most of which should be broken out according to lender and shown separately on the balance sheet. Banks, insurance companies, owners or shareholders, and trade creditors are some of the creditors to whom notes might be payable.

A note is a formal obligation, which means it has a definite maturity date and may have terms and conditions that require the company, or the creditor, to take certain actions once the note is in default. Your banker will expect you to pay these obligations as scheduled so that they remain current and in compliance; in addition, your banker will probably want to see copies of the notes or the agreements that govern the notes to review the consequences of a failure to keep these notes current. The banker might even prepare a compliance schedule, analyzing your financials every month, quarter, or year, depending upon the terms of the note and the frequency of your statements, to be sure you're still in compliance with the terms of the note and haven't, by a change in your financial condition, triggered a default in any of your loan payments.

The current portion of your long-term debt (payments due within twelve months of the statement date) should be shown in the current liabilities section of the statement. The rest of it should be in long-term liabilities and should be shown separately to make it easier to see and analyze. Debt under a revolving-credit agreement is normally classified as long-term debt if the expiration date of that agreement is more than twelve months away as of the date of the statement, even though the actual borrowings or take-downs under the revolving-credit agreement utilize a short-term instrument such as a demand note.

The banker's concern with all of these notes payable is that servicing them properly uses up cash flow. In addition, if you're not able to stay current, your other lenders may accelerate their notes, taking whatever steps they deem necessary to protect their interests, including taking collateral. That could significantly weaken your company as well as jeopardize the safety of your banker's loan. If you're heading for trouble, you ought to talk to your banker before it happens, not after.

Accounts Payable

Bankers regard your trade suppliers as an alternate source of credit for you—a poor source. You can increase a trade creditor's "loan" to your company by simply delaying payments while continuing to order from the supplier, meaning that most suppliers won't be aware, at least initially, that they've become your bankers. If you had asked your bank for additional money, your banker would have taken a look at your financials before giving you an answer. Trade creditors also get around to the same kind of analysis, but in many cases not until after you have already "borrowed" the extra funds from them.

Trade payables are therefore an important indicator of how well you're doing. If your finances are getting at all tight, many bankers will check you out in the trade, contacting your principal creditors or getting updated Dun & Bradstreet or other credit reports. They may also compare the level of your accounts payable from one statement date to the next. Bankers know that "borrowing" from your supplier is a source of easy and interest-free credit, and they look for rising payables as a good first sign that something may be wrong with your cash flow.

Accruals

Accruals typically include things like salaries that are due but unpaid as of statement date. Most bankers like to see accruals on a statement because it means that the financials are being prepared on an accrual basis, not a cash basis. Cash basis statements reflect only transactions involving cash. They do not include accounts payable, accounts receivable, depreciation, or any other noncash entry. They therefore are incomplete financial statements and of limited value to the banker. Accrual statements are a far more comprehensive way of presenting a company's financial condition. Cash statements, used by many smaller firms because they're easier to prepare, tend to understate net worth considerably because they include neither receivables nor payables and because receivables are usually larger than payables. Their major shortcoming is their failure to portray a full picture of what's really going on; a customer's willingness to tolerate such poor quality information is always a disconcerting sign to a lender.

Subordinated Debt

Subordinated debt is debt that has subordinated some of its rights to those of other creditors. The result is that in the liquidation of a company, other creditors will receive payment (in part or in full, depending on the terms of the subordination) before the holders of subordinated debt receive payment. To most bankers, subordinated debt can be as good as equity. The more equity in the business, the more readily losses can be absorbed and still allow for payment of creditors in full in the event the company is liquidated.

The best kind of subordinated debt for bankers is that which is subordinated solely to the banker. When that's the case, it's really better than equity because, in the event of liquidation, whatever the subordinated debt holder receives in payment is turned over to the banker, thereby reducing the banker's loss.

Net Worth

Net worth, also called capital or equity, is one of the first things a banker looks at. Most bankers believe that when the going gets tough, the owner with a large investment in the company is most likely to stay and nurse the company back to good health; bankers fear that if the owner has little or nothing invested, it's easier to walk away, leaving the bank and other creditors holding the bag. A large net worth also provides more margin for error, greater ability to absorb losses, and more time to make changes and turn the company around.

As vital as net worth is, it does not represent a firm and precise value, because it is based on a number of factors that may have been calculated in any number of ways. Despite its weaknesses, net worth is still a key item. Bankers calculate debt-to-net-worth ratios (discussed in the next chapter) in an attempt to measure a company's margin for error or its staying power. Those ratios, which compare the creditor's investment in the business with the owner's investment, are regarded by many as reliable early indicators of upcoming problems; as debt ratios rise, bankers and others start asking if a company's assets are really worth as much as the balance sheet suggests.

Bankers feel good when they see a lot of net worth. But they know how easily net worth can evaporate, so don't be surprised if they regard your net worth with a jaundiced eye until you satisfy them that it is in fact as real as it appears.

CHAPTER PERSPECTIVE

Financial statements give an impression of precision that can be misleading. Bankers know this and view a balance sheet a good deal more conservatively than you might, asking not what it's worth today but what it might be worth if the borrower ever gets into financial difficulty. When bankers grill you about your figures, they're really trying to satisfy themselves that things will really turn out to be what they appear to be.

Financial Statements: The P&L and the Ratios

INTRODUCTION AND MAIN POINTS

This chapter looks at the income and expense statement, also called the profit and loss statement (P&L), from a banker's point of view and then discusses how the banker uses ratios to analyze both the balance sheet and the P&L.

After studying the material in this chapter:

■ You'll have a good idea of what bankers look for in your income and expense statement and what they regard as a satisfactory level of profit.

■ You'll understand how a banker uses comparative spreadsheets to get a sense of where your company has been and where it's headed.

■ You'll know what kind of ratio tests bankers are likely to use in analyzing your statements and how those ratios may influence their thinking about you, your company, and your loan.

THE NEED FOR PROFITS

If the balance sheet is a still photograph of your business at a particular point in time, then the P&L is something more dynamic, for it shows what you did with the business during the period of time preceding the photograph. Or at least, it tries to show that. As you've seen from our discussion of balance sheets, financial statements, with their neatly arrayed columns of finite figures, involve many assumptions and therefore may not always portray your company as accurately as they appear to.

So it is with the P&L. The profits you show are dependent on factors such as which method of accounting for inventory costs is used, how soon you recognize bad inventory or receivables and write them off, what you do at year-end to increase or decrease income or expense for window-dressing purposes or for tax purposes, and how quickly you write off plant and equipment.

The underlying question is whether or not there is a right amount of profit to show. And the answer is no—unless you're a larger, publicly-held company, in which case the right profit has more to do with what the marketplaces for stocks are looking for from other publicly held companies in terms of return on equity and earnings per share.

Assuring the Banker

When bankers look at your P&L, they're looking for assurance that your business is at least solvent. They want to know if you're generating enough cash to keep yourself current with all your other creditors; if you're profitable enough to meet your normal equipment needs, or to expand plant and equipment and working capital so that you can capitalize on new sales opportunities; if you're able to meet your own lifestyle objectives without unduly burdening the business; and finally, if you've got a sufficient margin for error. If your profits aren't achieving all those things, then your banker may start thinking about shoring up the bank's position in anticipation of a battle later on with other creditors over who gets how much of what's left if you go bankrupt. So you need not just profits, but enough profits to meet the needs of the business.

To Purchase New and Replacement Equipment

A major claim on profits is simply maintaining the status quo. Equipment wears out and needs to be replaced; in an inflationary economy, that replacement probably will cost more than the original. You need profits to fund the difference in cost.

It's possible that an exact duplicate of the original equipment won't meet your needs at replacement time; you may need more sophisticated equipment that works faster or makes a better product. Then your replacement is going to cost more, even if there has been no inflation. If you decide to upgrade equipment before it wears out rather than replace it, to keep up with the competition and with customer demands, you'll be replacing equipment before you've had time to depreciate it fully, adding to your cash shortfall when you do get new equipment.

The cash shortfalls incurred in our example could be funded by borrowing the money if your profits didn't cover them. But if you borrowed the money while your company is making no profit at all and while you're fully funding your depreciation expense to provide money for replacement equipment, you have no source for the money to repay the loan. So borrowing to fund all or part of your replacement costs doesn't really alter the need for profits at all; it just alters the timing of the need for profits.

To Provide for Expansion

Company expansion can involve anything from doing more of what the company already does to entering new territory or new product or service lines or acquiring part or all of other companies. It's hard to imagine an expansion that doesn't require more cash—and if that cash doesn't come from the owners, then, short of borrowing it, the only remaining source of it is the profit margin. Borrowing can create its own problems; many companies have gone bankrupt because, when profits weren't adequate to underwrite the increased working capital and equipment needs that went with its successes, they borrowed repeatedly until they either could no longer service the debt or ran into an unexpected difficulty.

Rising sales create another and less obvious need for profits—a need to build up inventory and receivables. Although that buildup will be offset to some degree by an increase in payables, there will be a net increase in company funds tied up in working capital. On top of that, that increased working capital is not depreciated, as you would depreciate a piece of equipment. Without the depreciation, there is nothing to focus attention properly on the need to fund an investment which can be as long term as any equipment purchase but which, unlike a major purchase, can occur in small increments over time.

The analogy to an equipment purchase can be carried a bit further. Like a major piece of equipment, inventory may become outdated or old-fashioned before the increased investment in working capital has generated enough profits to equal or exceed the investment.

To Achieve Your Desired Lifestyle

One of the lines on a typical bank spreadsheet calls for total salary and benefit expense of the company; however, the salaries and benefits banks are most interested in are usually those of the owners of the business. While the banker's concern is that the principals may be depriving the business of money that it needs, it's surprising how often, especially in very young and very small businesses, the amount of money taken out by the principal and other members of the family is quite small. While the hope is that over time that poor salary situation will be corrected, many times that is not the case. For some entrepreneurs, that's a disappointment; for others, being their own boss makes up for the lack of financial return.

Others, however, take out large salaries from the company, plus money for cars for family members, club memberships, frequent "business" trips, salary advances, loans, homes or condos in resort areas for entertainment use, excessive rents for land or buildings owned by the principals, or other personal uses. All of which is fine as long as the business is doing well. But it can become a major problem, from a banker's point of view, when company fortunes change and cash flow begins to be inadequate; it's difficult for principals to cut back on a style of living they've come to enjoy and to reduce their generosity to family members.

To protect the bank's interest in the company, bankers sometimes include requirements in formal loan agreements that frequently contain limitations on salary payable to the owners or to all officers. There may also be dollar or percentage restrictions on salary increases from year to year. If a default should occur under the loan agreement, salaries are one of the first areas bankers scrutinize, although they are careful not to overdo it and risk driving the principals away, since the owners are usually the key to a successful revival of any company.

INCOME AND EXPENSES
Income

For most companies, income is pretty straightforward. It's usually shown as a gross figure from which rebates, discounts, and similar items are deducted to arrive at a figure called net sales. Net sales is regarded by bankers as the "real" sales figure and is used as the basis for a number of sales ratio tests. If there's anything conditional about sales, bankers want to know about that. Are there, for example, guarantees which could come back to haunt the company in later months or years? Is inventory being sent out on consignment and being called sales? If your company is a contractor and receives progress payments, could receivables or revenues already received be jeopardized by your failure to meet deadlines or quality testing?

Sales income is the lifeblood of any company; it's another one of those "first things" that a banker looks at. Rising sales are normally the sign of a company that is doing well.

After bankers look at sales, the next "first thing" they look at is net income. They want to see if profit increases are keeping pace with sales increases. If they're not, a quick look for any unusual, one-time expenses that may have caused the profits lag is followed by a hard look at all the other expense categories to determine the reason for the lag.

Expenses

Cost of goods sold is probably the most difficult of all expenses to understand and state properly. The cost of goods sold depends largely on the value given to inventory at the beginning and the end of the time covered by the P&L. Those values in turn are the result of the combination of actual cost figures, added value figures, and adjustments up or down to reflect market values. There are many subjective elements in inventory valuation and therefore in the cost of sales figure as well. The same concerns that move bankers to look closely at value shown for inventory on the balance sheet compel them to evaluate carefully figures for cost of goods sold.

In many cases, bankers' best defense against the uncertainty of the data in both balance sheets and P&Ls are the spreadsheets and the ratio tests that are discussed next.

SPREADSHEETS

A credit analyst's best friend is a spreadsheet or, as it is more formally called, a comparative analysis sheet or a comparative spreadsheet. The key word is comparative. The analyst transfers all the figures on a company balance sheet and P&L into columns on the spreadsheet, preparing one spreadsheet for the balance sheet, one for the P&L, and one or more for cash-flow analyses and for the various ratios that the analyst calculates. While some banks still prepare spreadsheets on paper, many others use computers for the chore. Each vertical column on a spreadsheet contains balance sheet and P&L data for a particular period of time or as of a particular statement date. Each time a new statement is received from a customer, the appropriate data is entered in the next column to the right. The result is a series of vertical columns which, when scanned horizontally, show what cash, or receivables, or sales, or profits were for each period. For interim (monthly or quarterly) figures, a new sheet is usually started each fiscal year. Information may be presented for each month or quarter or on a year-to-date basis, or both. In addition, there is a spreadsheet containing fiscal statements that may go back many years and thus provide an excellent comparative history of the company.

Presenting similar periods of time side by side makes it easy for a banker to compare performances and to spot trends. In particular, the banker looks for trends that signal changing needs and opportunities for the company, as well as for signs of possible problems in repaying existing loans. In larger banks, the transfer and comparison of data are done in credit departments; analysts, some quite experienced, others training to be loan officers, prepare narrative reports on the borrower and on the borrower's industry. In smaller banks, loan officers may do the transfer and spread work themselves. In the smallest banks, which tend to be understaffed for this kind of work, the spreadsheet work may never get done at all, which means, if you go back to the notion that you will do best when the banker knows and understands your company, that you are more likely to fare poorly with a small bank; uncertainty in the mind of the banker produces smaller loans, harsher terms and conditions, and even turndowns.

For the bankers who do use spreadsheets, they are marvelous tools for analysis. Most bankers prefer to look at them instead of the actual financial statements. And there's no reason why you shouldn't set up your own figures on a similar basis for your own analysis. Trends, both good and bad, jump out at the analyst and become the basis for good discussion between borrower and lender. Similarly, interim spreadsheets reveal seasonal patterns and make comparison with prior seasons easy and meaningful.

RATIOS

There is no one set of ratios that is applicable to all companies, but the overall theories are much the same. The ratios are intended to help analysts discern change and to test the quality of the figures on the balance sheet and the P&L. You should ask your banker to show you the ratios the bank prepares on your company; you might even consider doing all or most of them yourself before you bring the figures to the bank. Having them done in advance allows you to anticipate your banker's reactions and is convincing evidence that you're on top of what's going on financially within your company. You might even discover that your banker's analyses aren't as complete as they ought to be.

You might be surprised at the number of pages of ratio analysis that just a few figures from your balance sheet and your P&L can generate. You should go over these data with your banker to satisfy yourself that the figures the bank is using are valid. Even if you're not satisfied with the bank's approach, you will at least have a clearer idea of the way the bank analyzes your company and therefore be better able to present your case.

Common Ratios

Common ratios relate balance-sheet and P&L items to one common figure. Total assets and net sales each are defined as equal to 100 percent; everything else on the balance sheet is expressed as a percent of total assets and every line on the P&L is expressed as a percent of net sales. Such ratios are helpful in comparing data when the values of the underlying numbers are changing rapidly, as in a company experiencing rapid growth. They are also helpful in comparing the figures of two different companies. The underlying figures can be vastly different but the relationships of the various components should be similar, regardless of size; differences in relationships invite further investigation and understanding. Many of the questions your banker asks of you may stem from differences between your ratios and those of a comparable firm.

Some Traditional Ratios

Lenders rely on ratio analysis for the answers to some fundamental questions about a loan applicant's financial condition, including the following: 1) What is the borrower's current solvency? 2) How does this compare to recent past performance? 3) How does this borrower measure up against companies of similar size in the same industry? A ratio for any company can be compared to: 1) the company's industry average, as reported by Robert Morris Associates' *Annual Statement Studies;* 2) another company in the same industry, also using RMA data; 3) the same ratio for the company in prior years. Composite ratios for different industries are also published by Dun & Bradstreet, Inc., and Standard & Poor's. These references can be found in most college and public libraries.

The ratios used most often in credit analysis fall into three broad categories: leverage ratios, liquidity ratios, and coverage ratios. Leverage ratios (also called solvency ratios) measure the degree to which a business is dependent on borrowed funds, such as the following:

$$\text{liabilities to tangible net worth ratio} = \frac{\text{total liabilities (current debt + fixed debt)}}{\text{tangible net worth}}$$

This ratio measures the amount of capital contributed by creditors or investors in a business. As the number approaches 100, the creditors' interest approaches the owners' investment in the business. Another useful ratio is the following one:

$$\text{fixed assets to tangible net worth ratio} = \text{fixed assets/tangible net worth}$$

This ratio shows the relationship between investment in plant and equipment and the owners' capital. As the ratio increases, less capital is available for payroll, current expenses and other working capital needs. Highly leveraged companies are more vulnerable to business downturns than companies with lower debt-to-worth ratios, although the amount of leverage can vary by industry group.

There are many liquidity ratios, all of which try to measure the adequacy of current assets and a company's ability to pay its current obligations. Key liquidity ratios include the following:

$$\text{current ratio} = \frac{\text{current assets}}{\text{current liabilities}}$$

$$\text{quick ratio} = \frac{\text{cash + marketable securities + accounts receivable}}{\text{current liabilities}}$$

$$\text{working capital turnover} = \frac{\text{net sales}}{\text{current assets} - \text{current liabilities}}$$

Coverage ratios measure the ability to service debt, including bank loans. A high ratio indicates the borrower would be able to make loan interest payments with little difficulty. An example is the debt-coverage ratio, which compares pretax earnings to loan interest expense.

$$\text{debt coverage ratio} = \frac{\text{earnings before interest and taxes (EBIT)}}{\text{annual interest expense}}$$

Another widely used coverage ratio measures a company's ability to pay currently maturing debt.

$$\text{current debt coverage} = \frac{\text{net profit + depreciation}}{\text{current portion of long-term debt}}$$

The current ratio and the quick ratio are probably two of the oldest ratios around. Analysts used to consider a current ratio of two to one ideal. It may still be for many companies, but for many others, it's more important to observe how that ratio changes from one period to another. It's a measure of liquidity and rests on the notion that if you had to sell all your current assets, as in a liquidation, you'd have sufficient proceeds from that sale to pay off not only all current liabilities but all or a significant portion of the rest of your liabilities as well. The current ratio assumes full value for all the current assets; that of course is its weakness, since the value of assets for an ongoing concern can be quite different from those of one in liquidation.

The quick ratio is calculated by dividing current assets, excluding inventory, by current liabilities. If two to one is the classic value for the current ratio, then one to one is the traditional proper figure for the quick ratio. It's better than the current ratio as a measure of liquidity, since it removes inventory, one of the stickiest of assets, from the equation. The liquidation values of cash and receivables (usually most of what's left after inventory is eliminated) is considerably less than their worth in an ongoing company, but they exist nevertheless. (The cash, come liquidation day, is likely to be entirely gone, and many of the receivables are likely to be in dispute or will not be honored.) As was the case with the current ratio, the period-to-period changes in the quick ratio should be of more interest to you than the absolute value of the ratio itself.

Not a ratio, but a figure of interest, is working capital—current assets minus current liabilities. This figure represents your company's long-term investment, net of what others have invested, in cash, receivables, inventory, and other miscellaneous assets; it fluctuates moderately from period to period, generally staying within a fairly close range unless other events take place. Working capital figures do not change, however, if short-term loans are used to finance larger inventory or receivables or to pay down trade debt. For proper analysis, therefore, the working capital figure and the current and quick ratios should be used together.

Turnover Ratios

Turnover ratios—sales (usually net sales) divided by receivables, cost of goods sold divided by inventory, and cost of goods sold divided by payables—are like quick temperature readings. Usually expressed in days, they're rough indicators of whether your customers are slowing up their payments to you, whether your inventory is growing in relation to your sales, or whether you're slowing up on your payments to your suppliers. You may already do this kind of testing of your figures on your own, but if you're not, you ought to; if you discover significant period-to-period changes, you ought to investigate thoroughly.

Every company should age its receivables, breaking them down into current receivables and showing separately those past due for 30 days, 60 days, and 90 days or more. When the age of your receivables starts to grow, it can mean some of your customers are running into problems or that you're not following up on your tardy accounts as aggressively as you should. Slow receivables are worth checking into, since they translate rapidly into interest paid to your banker, an expense you want to minimize.

Dividing sales by working capital is another turnover calculation you may find interesting. It tells you how often your investment in working capital is turning over. As a general rule, the faster you turn over any investment, whether working capital or a piece of equipment, the better your profits are likely to be. Putting it differently, the more sales you generate with any investment, the sooner you'll be able to pay for it. There's no point in buying equipment or working capital and not putting it to good and active use. Dividing sales by working capital is a way for you to measure your own performance in this area. Your banker will be doing it anyway; it's probably a normal part of the output of his software package.

P&L Ratios

You can calculate just about any item on the P&L as a percent of sales (usually net sales after discounts, rebates, etc.). The most popular such calculations are:

■ gross margin (sales minus cost of goods sold)
■ SG&A (salaries plus general and administration costs, but excluding depreciation)
■ margin (SG&A plus all other costs, excluding depreciation)
■ net margin (net income)

Changes in any of these ratios from one period to another mean that there have been increases or decreases in one or more of the components of those ratios and invite immediate research to find out why.

Many analysts also calculate return on total assets (net income as a percent of total assets) and net income as a percentage of net worth. Return on total assets shows how well you're doing with what you've got; when it's used to compare your company's performance with that of another company, the comparison can be skewed if both companies don't have the same relative amounts of capital.

The net worth calculation is particularly interesting because you can readily compare ROEs between companies, assuming that the net worth figures are reasonably accurate representations of the value of each company's balance sheet. Remember, though, that for many small companies, the real ROE is closely related to the salary line. For businesses that are not providing reasonable salaries to their owners, the ROE figure ought to be reduced, even changed to a loss, in order to reflect a more accurate measure of ROE. Conversely, for the company that is providing its owners with handsome salaries and benefits, ROE ought to be adjusted upward.

One additional use of ROE is comparing it with the return on your original investment (ROI), net income as a percent of that investment, and then comparing those with what you might have earned had you just put your money in government securities or some other investments instead.

Cash Flow Analysis

The traditional way to look at cash flow is to add back depreciation expense to net income, since depreciation, while a real expense, does not represent a cash outlay. The problem with that approach is that there are a number of other things going on in your financial statements that also have an impact on how much cash you will have at the end of the accounting period. This leads bankers to use a variety of different cut-off points or cash flow figures, all of which are helpful but no one of which is definitive.

The cash flow analysis begins with the figure for net sales, the source of all or nearly all of the company's cash flow. Then come the adjustments. For example, as your receivables or inventory rise, so does the amount of cash you use. Just the reverse is true for your accounts payable. So the banker or the analyst adjusts the traditional cash flow figure by subtracting from it the money you invested in additional inventory or receivables or the money you spent to reduce your accounts payable or your accruals. To the extent you reduce your inventory or receivables or let your payables or accruals grow, the analyst also adds the appropriate amount to the traditional cash flow figures. (Note that changes in current bank debt are not included at this point.) The cash flow figure, as refined up to this point, shows the impact on cash flow of the company's day-to-day operation. Remember, though, that this figure can be impacted significantly by year-end or period-end adjustments or flukes that affect the company's cash position.

The next refinement in cash flow involves the impact upon cash flow of the purchase or sale of other assets, mostly equipment changes. The analyst reduces the cash flow by the cost of equipment purchased or adds to cash flow an amount equal to the cash received for assets sold. The resulting figure shows what the cash flow would have been had there been no increases or decreases in short-term or long-term debt. If the cash flow is positive at this point, it shows the extent to which debt has been reduced; if the cash flow is negative, it reveals the company's need for outside financing during the period.

The next step is to show how the company resolved those financing requirements. Separate lines indicate the change in short-term debt, long-term debt, and in capital (also a form of financing). After including those changes, the final cash flow figure should equal the change in cash position for the period involved.

Then the banker begins asking questions. Did the company, for example, finance equipment with short-term or long-term borrowings? Was its use of term debt a resolution of working capital imbalances that had developed over the course of prior years? Did the company depend too heavily on financing by the bank or by the trade, or both? Did it use bank debt to pay out equity to the owners, or did the owners put money into the business to reduce dependence on bank debt? The significant thing here is not the change in cash position but what caused it to move.

Ability to Service Debt

Bankers calculate your ability to service debt by dividing your income before taxes by the interest paid during the year. One-to-one is pretty close; anything over that adds cushion. If the ratio is less than one-to-one, the chances are good that you met your interest payments by borrowing money from someone.

If the company is making regular principal reductions on long-term debt, the analysts will include the principal paid as well the interest and see how the ability to service both principal and interest stacks up. Again, one-to-one is barely passing and leaves you little room for error; one-and-one-quarter-to-one or one-and-a-half-to-one is much better.

A variation on that approach is to take traditional cash flow (net income plus depreciation) and divide that by the payments made on long-term debt. Both are a measure of the company's margin of safety—and therefore, the bank's.

Debt Ratios

Debt ratios relate indebtedness to capital. They are used to divide either total liabilities, including all current debt, or long-term liabilities by net worth (tangible net worth, the net worth shown on the balance sheet minus intangible assets, such as goodwill). An additional ratio might add any subordinated debt to the net worth figure; a separate ratio might treat the subordinated debt as part of total indebtedness, since it, like other debt, must be paid off at some time in the future. In large companies, the subordinated debt is often publicly held debt; in smaller companies, it is often money owed to one or more principals, a guarantor, or perhaps a prior owner.

Debt ratios show how much the shareholders have invested in the company compared to all other creditors. The banker, of course, likes to see plenty of capital and prefers that owners have a large stake in the business. Debt equal to twice the capital is a fairly common figure; some borrowers go as high as four-to-one, although normally a bank will lend to such a company only on a secured basis.

Industry Averages

It's natural to want to know what kind of ratios other companies in your industry generate. If you fit into a readily identifiable category, your trade association may be able to help you. In addition, banks, through organizations such as Robert Morris Associates, generate common company data. The biggest problem with data such as Robert Morris Associates' annual statement studies is that many companies, large and small, have diversified, so that they cannot be readily compared to their competitors. In addition, many companies have sought special niches in the marketplace, niches that can alter the normal relationships of balance sheet and P&L figures.

If your bank has loan specialists and if your company fits into one of those specialties, your banker can probably give you a pretty good idea of what kinds of figures or ratios exist in the specialty without giving away competitive secrets. Failing that, your banker ought to be able to get additional figures through one or another of the bank's correspondent bankers.

General Considerations

Financial statements are usually based on period-end data, making them vulnerable to distortion from events that occur at or near the end of that period. If there are such distortions in your case, it's a good idea to tell your banker about them ahead of time so that they can be taken into account properly during the bank's analysis.

Discussions with your banker shouldn't be only a matter of your meeting the bank's requirements; they should provide opportunities for trading insights and opinions, helping you understand each other a little better. If it seems as though your banker has an insatiable appetite for figures and ratios, it's at least partly because financial statements are an imperfect way of telling you or your banker how healthy your company really is. If you can, you should feed your banker as much of the information requested as possible.

There are excellent software programs available; depending on your line of business, there may be programs designed specifically for companies like yours. If that is not the case, you'll probably be able to find other programs that can be easily modified to conform more closely to your needs.

Ask your accountant for help with computers and software or for a recommendation of someone qualified to guide you. There are numerous consultants available, and they too should be able to help get you up and running quickly without your going through a time-consuming, and potentially costly, trial-and-error process.

CHAPTER PERSPECTIVE

Lending is more an art than a science, and its practice can be highly subjective. The approach of any one loan officer is a product of past experience and current environment. Don't be deceived by the specific and precise nature of the numbers on your financials; loan officers regard many of them with suspicion and so should you.

It is important for you to become familiar with the approach used by your bank and your loan officer. Most loan officers have pet ratios or benchmarks that they use when they're analyzing credits; most loan officers have had plenty of loans go bad in the past and have learned that it's difficult to predict how all borrowers will behave when the going gets tough. That probably makes them rely more on the financials than perhaps they should, but at least it helps explain the apparent fascination that many loan officers seem to have for the financials.

The challenge for your banker is to be optimistic about the prospects for you and your company. The challenge for you is to provide good quality information so that the banker can properly assess your borrowing needs and your ability to repay. Remember, the banker is just another sales prospect. Fulfill your banker's analytic needs and need for assurance, and you'll have a much better chance of making the sale you're after.

When Your Loan Request Is Turned Down

INTRODUCTION AND MAIN POINTS

This chapter discusses loan turndowns and what you can do about them.

After studying the material in this chapter:
- You'll learn some of the reasons banks turn down loan requests.
- You'll learn what options you have available to you after your banker has said no.

THE TURNDOWN

It is rare that a request for a loan is turned down with a simple "no." If that ever happens to you, you should not leave it there. There have to be reasons for the turndown; you have a right to know what they are and to understand them. You may not agree with the reasoning of the loan officer or the loan committees, but you should at least know what it is.

Getting turned down on a loan request is an ego-bruising experience for some customers; for others, it's just the beginning of another round, disappointing perhaps, but not earth-shattering. Still others become enraged and rant and rave. Even for loan officers, saying "no" is a troubling experience. They may feel hurt pride, since most loan officers believe they know their bank well enough to predict accurately what they can get through and what they can't. If the bank has a bonus or commission system, a turndown can also represent a loss of dollars for the loan officer. Finally, since most officers enjoy getting customers the money they want, they experience no gratification in turndowns.

Some loan officers aggravate the customer's pain by failing to couch the turndown in proper and appropriate words or by seeming cold and uncaring. Others are understanding and try to find other ways of helping the customer. Some loan officers fail to give any indication that a loan request may be in trouble, so that during the preliminary discussions the customer has no idea that the request is doubtful and the turndown, when it comes, is a total surprise. Ideally, the customer ought to know early on whether a request is an easy one, a problematic one, or too close to call.

Loan requests can sometimes run into surprising resistance during the approval process, so that even though the customer has a pretty good feel for the way the loan officer felt, the final answer may be a surprise. A good loan officer, however, never blames the turndown on others but presents it as "the bank's position." If your banker blames senior loan officers or the committee, it may be a sign of weakness on the part of your loan officer, and it may well be time for you to start looking for a new banker—which you may have to do anyway if the rejection doesn't provide any reasonable alternatives.

AFTER THE TURNDOWN

A good loan officer never says "no" but rather searches for other ways to get the job done. Your loan officer's list of suggestions may include one or more of the following: Reducing the amount of the loan request, revising the repayment terms, providing collateral or more collateral, providing a guarantee (really another form of collateral), or abandoning, modifying, or delaying the project that gave rise to the request in the first place. It is important that you find out why those kinds of suggestions are being made. What were the shortcomings that produced the turndown? Was the proposed loan so large that it could not be serviced within a reasonable period of time? Or would it significantly distort your balance sheet or your cash flow? Why the need for more collateral, a guarantor, or a reduced loan amount? All the banker needs is assurance that the loan will be repaid; find out what's getting in the way of that assurance. Is it that yours is a new business, or that you're inexperienced in the field or in running a company, or that the company's line of business is widely regarded, at least by bankers, as a risky one?

Typically, you'll learn of your turndown over the phone, probably soon after a committee meeting, although the call could come after your loan officer has finished analyzing your credit or after a senior loan officer has said no. There are two things you need to do, one of them before you get off the phone. That is to make an appointment to visit your loan officer to review what's happened. The officer may try to beg off, but don't allow it. Set the date for several days later so that you have sufficient time for the second thing you need to do—reviewing the whole proposal from the point of view of a bank loan officer or credit analyst. Subject it to all the ratios and tests you think they might use. Test your own theories again, too. Do a "strong points and weak points" analysis. Write it out and be tough about it.

Loans normally get paid from cash flow generated by earnings or from the proceeds of asset liquidation or turnover. How realistic were your projections for earnings or cash flow? How large a margin for error did you provide? Is the banker's primary source of payment a sure thing, or is it based on wishful thinking? Where is the banker's alternate source of payment, the one that will pay the loan if the first set of assumptions doesn't work out? How solid is that source of payout? Is the repayment dependent upon everything going just right?

Getting Ready for the Next Bank

If, after you've done all this, you still feel you were right and they were wrong, at least you're ready for the second assault. But you need to go in there with a second purpose in mind—your alternate course of action if your appeal doesn't work. Once it's clear that you're not going to succeed, you should ask your loan officer what other banker in town, or in a town nearby, might be interested in your proposal. If you've been a customer of your present bank for any length of time, ask your loan officer for an introduction as well or the right to use your loan officer's name. Don't worry about the two of them getting together and talking about your company; that's going to happen anyway, since the second bank will want to know what went wrong with the first one.

In either event, ask the loan officer to coach you and to critique your proposal. Remember that your current banker is off the hook at this point, possibly relieved at the thought of sending you on your way and maybe even getting thanked for it. As a result, you may pick up some additional insights that didn't come out before. Pump your new coach for suggestions: "Is there more information I need? What's the matter with the collateral? Who could I get for a guarantor? Who might be interested in investing something in this business? What would you do in my position? How else can I get the money I need to realize on this opportunity?"

Another possible cause for your turndown may be that you are not a very convincing salesperson. This can be particularly important if you are already borrowing close to the maximum that your company in its situation is entitled to. If you haven't organized your material and your presentation well, your loan officer may not have gotten the entire picture or may have gotten it improperly. If you give the impression that you lack confidence, you may trigger similar feelings in your banker and in others. Remember, successful salesmanship means fulfilling customer needs. One way or another, you may not be doing that for your customer—the banker.

Going Over the Loan Officer's Head

If you think your loan officer hasn't done a good job for you or that another loan officer could have gotten the job done, you may decide to appeal to higher authority. But you ought to be sure of your ground, and you ought to be prepared to leave the bank if you do take this step. Going over your banker's head may not help your relationship at all and therefore jeopardize future loan requests. Some loan officers may not object at all, especially since you'll probably be talking to one of the people who joined in turning down your loan. If you think the personal chemistry between you and your loan officer is poor, or if the person in the chain of command to whom you will talk used to handle your account, still knows it well, and still has good and strong vibes about it, you may do well to appeal. Often a loan officer further up the chain of command says "no" to a junior officer and later, when confronted by a persuasive customer armed with determination and total knowledge of the business, changes a no vote to a yes vote so that the next time the same loan goes to committee, it sails through with no significant opposition.

WHEN YOUR LOAN GOES BAD

Open communication with your banker is essential if you want to maintain good relations. This is especially important when you are having financial problems. Avoiding your banker in times of difficulty will only cause further trouble because your loan officer will think you have something to hide. If you think you're going to miss a loan payment, get on the phone and tell your banker what's going on. Try to work out a new repayment schedule. If you've been truthful, your banker may be willing to renegotiate the loan and extend the loan term so you have a longer period to repay the debt.

Bankers really don't want to take possession of collateral or force you to sell collateral to repay the loan. The earlier you initiate the discussion, the better your chances for coming up with a repayment plan that works for you. If your financial situation is likely to remain the same, your banker may simply decide to *term out the debt,* extending the length of time you have to repay the loan. You will pay more in finance charges over this extended loan period, but you will have avoided worse consequences. In all cases, preventing problem loans is better than solving problem loans.

The alternative may be coming up with additional collateral or loan guarantees. When the outlook for continuing a business is uncertain, money may have to be raised from sale of collateral pledged. In more severe situations, the money raised from sale of collateral may not equal the amount owed the bank. Borrowers still have a legal obligation to repay the loan in full.

In rare cases a banker will agree to a renegotiated loan with a reduced principal, effectively reducing the loan amount. But there's a catch here. By law, the amount by which the loan is reduced is considered income to the borrower. The presumption is the borrower had the benefit of the full loan amount, regardless of any change in financial condition. The lender may agree to reduce the loan principal from $100,000 to $80,000. The debt forgiven, $20,000, is treated for accounting purposes as ordinary income and is subject to federal and state income taxes.

Far worse than having your loan request turned down is having your loan go bad. There isn't any precise point at which a loan becomes "bad." Ideally for the bank, as deterioration sets in, the loan changes from unsecured to secured, thereby protecting the bank's position. Frequently, however, the bank finds itself with an unsecured or partially secured loan because of its own errors, faulty documentation, slow response to changing conditions, or collateral that loses some or all of its value over time.

Within the bank, there's a gradually rising level of awareness that the loan is deteriorating. Usually the loan officer becomes aware of problems first, then committee members, board members, and finally the bank examiners. Some banks work with the borrower as things go downhill; the extent of such cooperation depends largely on how well you have kept your bank up to date on your situation. The bank's help may produce enough flexibility, or even additional loans, so that you have time to get your company turned around and on the mend again.

But if things continue to worsen, you're very likely to have a change in loan officer. Some banks think that once a credit reaches some undefined low point, it is time for a more objective and less involved loan officer, someone who has no pride of authorship in the loan, to step into the picture. This is particularly true in larger banks, which have a staff devoted solely to handling bad loans. The change for the borrower can be traumatic; such loan officers are usually referred to as work-out officers and typically have only one interest at heart—to minimize the damage to the bank. They are well-versed on the ins and outs of bankruptcy and do all they can to posture the bank as well as possible before that bankruptcy comes. A measure of the nature of the job is that most loan officers who become work-out officers never get back on the line as regular commercial loan officers; it is a scarring experience, that makes it difficult for them to put full confidence in their customers any more.

Other banks believe that working out a loan, or at least trying to, is an invaluable experience for a loan officer. This means that you'll still have the same loan officer, but you're likely to find that there's a major change in your working relationship. Your loan officer will be virtually without authority, and little or nothing will be changed or approved without going back through committee. Even then, much of what comes back from committee will not be to your liking.

Probably the best advice for any entrepreneur is to realize that despite the jam, the principal of the business is usually the person most likely to be able to work the company out of its hole. Whether this takes more loans, drastic cutbacks, or new investors, the owner is still the key. The company may hover on the brink of bankruptcy for months while creditors sort out their relative positions and discover who among them is strong, who's weak, and who's bluffing. Once creditors sort out their relative positions, if there's still enough cash flow to keep the company moving, the chances for survival begin to improve.

CHAPTER PERSPECTIVE

Loan analysis is anything but a precise science. What one bank or one loan officer turns down is often agreed to by the next. Every loan proposal is based upon assumptions about what is going to happen to your company. That perception in turn depends in large part on what has already happened and how well your company is believed to have responded to past problems and opportunities.

Those who regard a loan turndown as simply the beginning of the next round are taking the best approach. For them, the principal question is where that next round is going to take place—at their current bank or at a new bank. Do your homework, do it well, be a little flexible, and you may get all or nearly all of what you wanted in the first place.

When to Change Banks

INTRODUCTION AND MAIN POINTS

This chapter discusses some of the reasons a depositor or borrower might want to change banks.

After studying the material in this chapter:

■ You'll learn what might motivate customers to leave one bank for another.

■ You'll learn some of the pros and cons of having two banks instead of one.

■ You'll become aware of some of the dangers of moving with your loan officer from one bank to another.

REASONS FOR CHANGING BANKS

Access to financing is the number one reason small businesses give for selecting a bank. Where you do your banking is likely to be influenced by many other factors besides having convenient access to a loan or line of credit. Banking is a service business and it's your responsibility to manage that relationship. If for any reason you become dissatisfied with your bank, it's always a good idea to have a backup—another bank you can work with—before taking your accounts elsewhere. Seek out bankers you are not doing business with now. That acquaintance may come in very handy later on.

One of the most common reasons for changing from one bank to another, aside from being turned down on a loan request, is unhappiness over the interest rate you're getting from the bank, whether you're a depositor or a borrower.

No matter where you keep your deposits, there's almost always another bank around that is offering a higher rate. Even in the same town, rates differ from one bank to another, and different banks may offer the highest rate at different times. If you always go with the highest rate possible, you'll wind up moving your money back and forth and gradually earn a reputation for being a "hot" customer with no bank loyalty at all. If convenience and quality of service are the same from bank to bank, then jumping around won't make much difference at all; if convenience and service do vary, you'll have to weigh these factors against the extra one-eighth or quarter or half percent you'll be earning. One-eighth percent on $10,000 is $12.50 a year, or $125 on a $100,000 deposit. You have to decide if the incremental interest income is worth the hassle of frequent switches.

If it's the rate on your loan that is unsatisfactory, that's a different matter. The rate can be important and the difference in rates can be expensive, but there are other facets of your loan relationship that you should evaluate very carefully before switching to another bank. How much is it worth to you to have a bank which understands your credit needs and gets you the credit you need when you need it and on the terms and conditions you need? Rates may be one of the mostly hotly debated aspects of a loan, but, unless they're significantly out of line, they shouldn't be the determining factor in locating your loan relationship.

Another frequent cause of changes from one bank to another is solicitation by the second bank. Banks are highly competitive, and if you're a good customer at one bank, you've probably already discovered that there are other banks out there who'd be delighted to have your business. Banks call on prospects for years, waiting patiently for an opportunity to bid on any piece of business. The opportunity usually comes sooner or later, triggered by a new loan request, unhappiness with a loan officer, a dispute over rate, almost anything. There's no harm in having more than one bank make a bid for your business; competition can improve rates, terms, and conditions. But it can be a tough call, and unless there are significant differences between what your current bank wants and the new one wants, you probably ought to stay where you are. Most banks have a strong sense of loyalty, too, and appreciate long-time good customers; such factors are very often a key part of the discussion when a loan comes up for approval.

If you're not getting along well with your loan officer and there are no other loan officers in the bank who could substitute—and you're sure you're not part of the problem—then you may have a good reason for changing banks. A poor relationship with your loan officer can hurt the amount, the quality, and the price of the financing you're offered. But be careful—if you jump to another bank, your new loan officer may be no better, and may be even worse, than the one you have.

It's usually not wise to follow your loan officer from one bank to the next, particularly without checking out the change of banks very thoroughly. If your loan officer was in good standing at your current bank, the same is likely to be the case at the next bank as well. On the other hand, if your loan officer had been having problems at your current bank, those problems are likely to exist at the next bank as well, in which case, your loan officer might well be leaving that bank before too much longer. You're best off waiting a year or more before making this kind of move.

Sometimes, instead of changing banks, you can add another bank to your picture. If you can do that, and if you can keep yourself important to both institutions, you may create a beneficial situation for yourself, since neither of the two will quote any business to you without first considering what the other bank will do for the same business. But don't spread your business over two banks if it's going to be small potatoes in each bank. A $10,000 checking account in each of two banks, after activity costs, isn't going to generate as much banker interest in either of the two banks as one $20,000 account in one bank. And don't forget to consider the size of the banks involved. That $20,000 account might be much more important to a $10-million bank than it would be to a billion-dollar bank. The same thing goes for loans; one loan for $100,000 seems much more important to one bank than two $50,000 loans to either of two banks. Both banks certainly appreciate the business, but you may find that one and one adds up to less than two.

Other reasons for changing banks are:

■ a gossip in the bank or on the board. The stronger you feel about the confidentiality of your financials, the more important that gossip can be. A gossip on the board is not a frequent occurrence, but it does happen.

■ slow response to loan requests. Banks should be able to respond to loan requests within a week or so. But that week shouldn't start running until you've provided them with all the information they need.

■ your bank's demand for a guarantee that you don't want to give. But be careful: if you haven't had to give a guarantee and are now being asked for one, it may be a sign that your finances are going downhill. And that may be the worst time to change banks.

■ a turndown on a reasonable loan request. But again, be careful. If your turndown means your financial condition is slipping, leaving the bank that knows you well for one that doesn't could be the worst of moves.

WHAT TO LOOK FOR IN A BANK

First, look for a bank that is progressive and alert to changes in the community. Second, look for a bank with financial stability. You can learn a lot about a bank by reading its annual report to shareholders.

Also investigate publicly available information from the Federal Deposit Insurance Corporation and bank-rating agencies. Third, does the bank provide the services you need? Do bankers at that institution understand your problems? Are they familiar with your industry? If online access to your bank accounts is important, consider going with a bank offering both Internet banking and personal service from your account officer. You'll get "bricks and clicks" in your banking relationship—the best of both worlds.

Size of institution is irrelevant for many businesses. A number of large banks have very enterprising programs for small businesses, so don't write off the big banks. If your business is growing rapidly, your financing needs may someday outgrow your local community bank's ability to make those loans. On the other hand, small banks may offer more personal service. If your business is growing internationally and you need specialized service such as letters of credit, maybe you should go with a larger bank.

CHAPTER PERSPECTIVE

Changing banks is not something to be done lightly, especially if you're a borrower. Do a lot of checking around to be sure that the bank you're switching to will really be better for you than your current bank. And be sure that you yourself are not the primary problem and therefore the cause of your unhappiness. Encourage other banks to call on you and listen to what they have to offer—and then tactfully let your current bank know of your options. It may help improve the deal you're getting with your current bank.

If your account is big enough, spreading your relationship over two banks can be an excellent strategy. But you need to be big enough so that you make a difference. If one or both banks don't seem to pay much attention to your relationship, then you probably haven't gotten big enough for two banks and you'd be wasting what little impact you do have by dividing it in two.

Appendix
Sample Loan Forms

The following forms are not intended to constitute legal advice but are offered only as a guide to the kinds of terms and conditions that borrowers might encounter when entering into a loan agreement. Laws, regulations, and conventions vary from state to state, bank to bank, and lawyer to lawyer. Consequently, the forms vary widely as well. No company should sign any such document without first discussing its implications with an attorney.

LOAN AGREEMENT

This Loan Agreement by and between _____
_____ (hereinafter called "Borrower") and _____
_____ (hereinafter called "Bank") is executed in connection with a loan (hereinafter called "Loan") to be evidenced by a promissory note(s) (hereinafter called the "Note") which includes the following provisions and such other provisions as may be agreed upon by Borrower and Bank:

Amount of Note: $ _____ Date of Note: _____ Maturity: _____
                                    Term of Note: _____

In consideration of the Loan from Bank, the mutual covenants contained herein, and other good and valuable consideration, the Borrower hereby warrants, represents and agrees as follows:

1. WARRANTIES: The following warranties shall survive and continue after execution and delivery of this Agreement and the Bank's making the Loan:

  A. CAPACITY AND STANDING: The business operations of the Borrower are organized as a _____
_____ (indicate whether sole proprietorship, limited or general partnership or corporation).
    1. If the Borrower is a corporation, the Borrower is duly organized, validly existing and in good standing under the laws of _____ (State).
    2. (i) The Borrower has accomplished any fictitious name registration as required by law.
      (ii) If the Borrower is a partnership, the Borrower has also filed any necessary certificate of partnership. The names of all the general partners are: _____

  B. LITIGATION: There are no material pending or threatened actions or proceedings before any court or administrative agency, Federal or State, except as disclosed in a letter delivered by the Borrower to the Bank at or prior to the execution hereof.
  C. LIENS AND TAXES: The Borrower has filed all tax returns required to be filed and paid all taxes due pursuant to such returns or to any assessment received. The Internal Revenue Service has not asserted any liability for taxes in excess of those already paid by the Borrower and its property is free of any tax liens.
  D. BORROWER'S POWERS: The execution and performance of this Agreement, the Note, and the Related Loan Documents, if any, are within the Borrower's powers, have been duly authorized by appropriate corporate or partnership action, are not in contravention of the terms of Borrower's articles of incorporation, by-laws, regulations, close corporation agreements, partnership agreement or certificate or capital stock or any amendment thereof (such documents herein called "Organization Documents") and are not in contravention of any law or of any agreement to which Borrower is a party or by which it is bound.
  E. ASSET OWNERSHIP: All financial statements, profit and loss statements, statements as to ownership, and other statements heretofore or hereafter given to the Bank in connection with this Agreement, are or will be true and correct, subject to any limitation stated therein, and the Borrower is the owner of all property in which the Borrower has given or is giving a security interest to the Bank, free from all claims, liens, encumbrances and other security interests, and the Borrower will defend, at its sole expense, all such property against all claims and demands of all persons, firms and corporations other than the Bank at any time claiming the same or any interest therein.
  F. FINANCIAL CONDITION: Borrower's balance sheet and financial statements as of _____, furnished to Bank fairly present Borrower's financial condition and business operation at said date, and since said date there has been no material adverse change in its condition or operation.
  G. NOTICES: The Borrower manages its business activities or maintains its sole place of business at the following address: _____

2. AFFIRMATIVE COVENANTS: The Borrower will:

  A. REPAYMENT: Repay the Loan with interest thereon in accordance with the terms and conditions set forth in this Agreement and the Note.
  B. BUSINESS CONTINUITY: Continue operating in its present business form, will not materially reduce its business activities or engage in any new business activities without the prior written consent of the Bank, and will use the proceeds of the Loan only for the following purpose(s): _____

  C. CURRENT RATIO: Maintain current assets in excess of current liabilities by a least a ratio of _____ to 1.00. ("Current Ratio" shall mean the ratio of consolidated current assets to consolidated current liabilities determined in accordance with generally accepted accounting principles consistently applied.) If the Borrower is an individual, current business assets will be maintained excess of current business liabilities by a least the same amount.
  D. DEBT/WORTH RATIO: Maintain at all times a ratio of total liabilities to consolidated tangible net worth of not more than _____ to 1.00 ("total liability" shall mean as used herein all liabilities of the Borrower and its subsidiaries, if any, including capitalized leases, deferred taxes, other deferred sums, etc. in accordance with generally accepted accounting principals).
  E. FINANCIAL STATEMENTS: Furnish to the Bank within _____ days after the close of each of the Borrower's fiscal years, a balance sheet as of such year and a profit and loss and reconciliation of surplus statement for such year for the Borrower, said statements to be _____ (compiled, reviewed, or audited) and/or; furnish to the Bank within _____ days after the close of each _____ unaudited balance sheets and profit and loss statements for such period and such other data, financial or otherwise, as the Bank may request; and at all reasonable times permit a representative of the Bank to inspect the Borrower's business properties and make extracts from the Borrower's books and records. If Borrower is an individual, the Borrower will provide an annual personal financial statement in a form satisfactory to the Bank upon request, or at least annually.
  F. DISCHARGE OF LIENS AND TAXES: Pay all taxes, assessments and governmental charges upon the Borrower or against its properties prior to the date on which penalties are attached thereto, unless and to the extent only that the same shall be contested in good faith and by appropriate proceedings by the Borrower.
  G. COLLATERAL: As security for the Loan, deliver to the Bank the following collateral or duly executed security agreements, UCC's, Deed(s) of Trust, or such other documents as required by the Bank: _____
_____ (herein collectively called the "Related Loan Documents").
  H. INSURANCE: Maintain adequate fire (including so-called extended coverage), public liability, flood insurance and other insurance as the Bank may require, in such form and written by such companies satisfactory to the Bank, and will upon request of the Bank deliver to it the policies concerned. All policies covering property given as security for the Loan shall have loss payable clauses in favor of Bank.
  I. EXPENSES: Pay or reimburse the Bank for all reasonable out-of-pocket expenses of every nature including, but not limited to reasonable attorneys' fees, which Bank may incur in connection with this Agreement, and the Related Loan Documents, if any, or the collection of the indebtedness created hereunder.
  J. ERISA: The Borrower will use its best efforts to comply with all requirements of the Employee Retirement Income Security Act of 1974 "ERISA") and the provisions of all pension, profit-sharing, or other employee benefit plans now or hereafter established or maintained by the Borrower.
  K. DOCUMENTS: At the request of the Bank, the Borrower will supply the Bank with a copy of the Organization Documents.
  L. OTHER (Guarantors, Subordinations, etc.): _____
_____

3. NEGATIVE COVENANTS: Without the prior written consent of Bank, the Borrower will not:

A. BORROWINGS: Create or assume any obligation for money borrowed from any person, firm or corporation other than from the Bank.

B. GUARANTIES: Endorse, guarantee or become surety for the obligations of any person, firm or corporation, except that the Borrower may endorse checks or other instruments for deposit or collection in the ordinary course of business.

C. ENCUMBRANCES: Mortgage, pledge or otherwise encumber any of Borrower's property, real or personal, now owned or hereafter acquired, or permit any lien or security interest to exist thereon except liens: (i) for taxes and assessments not delinquent or being contested in good faith, (ii) of mechanics or materialmen with respect to obligations not overdue or being contested in good faith, (iii) resulting from deposits to secure payments of worker's compensation or other social security obligations or to secure the performance of bids or contracts in the ordinary course of business, (iv) in favor of the Bank, or (v) if the Borrower is an individual, existing on the Borrower's residential property on the date of this Agreement.

D. ADVANCES: Make any loans or advances to others.

E. INVESTMENTS: Invest any of its assets, or if Borrower is an individual any of its business assets, in securities other than direct obligations of the United States Government, commercial bank paper or certificates of deposit issued by the Bank.

F. SELL OR ASSIGN: Sell or assign any accounts receivable, with or without recourse; sell, transfer or assign any other assets, or if the Borrower is an individual any of its business assets, except in the ordinary course of business; or enter into any merger or consolidation with any person, firm or corporation; or alter or amend the Borrower's capital structure or business form.

G. DIVIDENDS: If the Borrower is a corporation, the Borrower will not declare or pay dividends in excess of $_____ in any fiscal year of the Borrower, except stock dividends or make any distribution of its assets to its shareholders, or redeem, purchase or otherwise acquire for value any of its outstanding shares of capital stock.

H. EXPENDITURE(S): Invest in any consecutive twelve-month period in capital assets used in or applicable to the Borrower's business in an aggregate amount in excess of $_____.

4. DEFAULT: In addition to the terms contained in the Note or any Related Loan Documents the following events shall be "Events of Default" hereunder:

a. Default by the Borrower in the payment of any principal of, or interest, on the Note when and as same shall become due and payable, whether at maturity, by acceleration, or otherwise; or

b. Default by Borrower in the payment of any of its debt (other than that evidenced by the Note) when and as same shall become due and payable; or

c. Any representation or warranty made or any financial statement or other information furnished by the Borrower or any officer or representative of it in connection with the execution and delivery of this Agreement, the Note or any Related Loan Document, or in any certificate furnished pursuant hereto shall prove to be false at any time in any material respect; or

d. Default by the Borrower in the due performance of any term, provision or agreement contained herein, in the Note (other than for the payment of principal or interest), or in any Related Loan Document or other instrument of security for the Note to be performed by it and such default shall continue unremedied for 30 days after notice thereof has been given to the Borrower by the Bank; or

e. The Borrower or any endorser, co-maker or guarantor with respect to the Note, shall become involved in financial difficulties as evidenced by: (i) making an assignment for the benefit of creditors; or commence any similar debtor relief proceeding, whether judicial or otherwise; (ii) consent to or application for the appointment of a trustee, interim trustee, custodian or receiver for all or a major portion of its property; (iii) the commencement of any action or proceeding under any other federal or state bankruptcy, insolvency, composition, debtor relief, reorganization or other similar law, or have such a proceeding commenced against any of them and either have an order of insolvency or reorganization entered against any of them or have the proceeding remain undismissed or unstayed for 60 days; (iv) entry of a final judgment for the payment of money against any of them in excess of $_____ and the same shall not be discharged within 30 days of its entry, or an appeal or proceeding for review shall not be taken within said time and a stay of execution pending such appeal shall not be obtained; (v) death, dissolution or suspension of the corporation charter or of the partnership; insolvency or failure or suspension of the usual business of any of them; (vi) the issuance of any attachment, garnishment, execution, federal tax levy, or other process or seizure against any of their property; or

f. The failure to pledge or hypothecate hereunder additional security when and as demanded by the Bank; or

g. Bank shall deem itself insecure, in good faith, believing that the prospect of payment of the Note or any other indebtedness owed to the Bank; or performance under this Agreement or any instrument providing security for the Note, is impaired.

If any one or more of the foregoing Events of Default shall happen, the Bank may, at any time, without notice to the Borrower, declare the unpaid principal of and interest on the Note to be immediately due and payable and such principal of and interest on the Note shall thereupon become and be immediately due and payable, without presentment, demand, protest or notice of any kind, all of which are hereby expressly waived by the Borrower, and the Bank may take such additional action as provided by law.

5. ADDITIONAL TERMS, DELETIONS AND EXCLUSIONS: The Borrower agrees to additional provisions, deletions and/or exclusions as follows: _____

_____

6. MISCELLANEOUS:

a. Paragraph headings are for reference only and shall otherwise be disregarded.

b. No waiver hereunder shall be effective unless in writing. No delay in exercising any right shall operate as a waiver thereof. A waiver on any one occasion shall not be a waiver of any right or remedy on any future occasion. This Agreement will terminate when all obligations of the Borrower to the Bank have been paid in full and the Bank shall not be obligated to advance any additional funds to the Borrower. This Agreement shall be governed by the laws of the State of West Virginia.

IN WITNESS WHEREOF and intending to be legally bound hereby, the Borrower has executed and delivered this Loan Agreement this _____ day of _____, 20_____.

_____   _____
(Name of Bank)   (Name of Corporation or Partnership)

By: _____   By: _____

Its: _____   Its: _____

GUARANTY AGREEMENT

IN CONSIDERATION of a loan by _____

_____ (hereinafter "Bank") to _____

_____ (hereinafter "Borrower") in the principal amount of_____

_____ Dollars

($_____), together with interest thereon, evidenced by Borrower's promissory note

(hereinafter "Note") dated _____ payable to the order of Bank, and in consideration of all other loans, advances, discounts or credits heretofore or hereafter granted by Bank to Borrower and in order to enable Borrower to maintain the Note and all such loans, advances, discounts or credits, the undersigned GUARANTOR(S) jointly and severally guarantee absolutely and unconditionally the prompt satisfaction when due, whether by acceleration or otherwise, of the Note and each and every other obligation of Borrower to Bank, now existing or hereafter arising, together with such interest as may accrue thereon, whether such indebtedness is incurred as principal, guarantor or endorser, is direct or indirect, absolute or contingent, original, renewed or extended, secured or unsecured, or is incurred by Borrower alone or jointly and/or severally with another or others (all of the aforementioned Note and other obligations being hereinafter collectively referred to as OBLIGATIONS).

Guarantor(s) jointly and severally agree that if any of the Obligations are not satisfied when due, Guarantor(s)will, upon demand by Bank, forthwith satisfy such Obligations or, if the maturity thereof shall have been accelerated by Bank, Guarantor(s) will forthwith satisfy all Obligations of Borrower. No such satisfaction shall discharge the liability of Guarantor(s) hereunder until all Obligations have been satisfied absolutely and in full. The liability of Guarantor(s) shall be reinstated and revived, and the rights of Bank shall continue, with respect to any amount at any time paid on account of any Obligation which shall thereafter be required to be set aside, all as though such amount had not been paid. Guarantor(s) jointly and severally further agree to pay Bank, upon demand, all losses and reasonable costs and expenses, including attorneys' fees, that may be incurred by Bank in attempting to cause the Obligations to be satisfied or in attempting to cause satisfaction of Guarantors' liability under this Agreement. Guarantor(s) further agree to provide Bank detailed financial statements annually, or upon request.

Guarantor(s) consent that Bank may exchange, release or surrender to Borrower or to any guarantor, pledgor or grantor any collateral, or waive, release, subordinate or fail to perfect and maintain any security interest or lien, in whole or in part, now or hereafter held as security for any of the Obligations; waive or delay the exercise of any of its rights or remedies against Borrower or any other person or entity, including without limitation any Guarantor(s); release Borrower or any other person or entity, including without limitation any Guarantor(s); renew, extend, modify, release, compromise or surrender any of the Obligations or any agreement or instrument evidencing the same; apply payments by Borrower, the Guarantor(s), or any other person or entity to any of the Obligations and in whatever order Bank elects; and take or not take any action in any proceeding affecting any of the Obligations or any collateral pledged to secure the Obligations.

Guarantor(s) waive all notices with respect to this Agreement or any of the Obligations, including without limitation notice of Bank's acceptance of this Agreement or its intention to act or its action in reliance hereon; the present existence or future incurring of any of the Obligations or any terms or amounts thereof or any change therein; any default by Borrower or any surety, pledgor, grantor of security or guarantor, including without limitation any of the Guarantor(s); and the obtaining or release of any guaranty, security agreement, pledge, assignment or other security for any of the Obligations.

Guarantor(s) waive notice of presentment, demand, protest, notice of dishonor and default, notice of non-payment, protest in relation to any instrument evidencing any of the Obligations, and any other demands and notices required by law, except as such waiver may be expressly prohibited by law.

Guarantor(s) waive in favor of Bank any claim, defense, right and offset which Guarantor(s) may have at any time against Borrower or any other party liable for all or any part of the Obligations, or against any assets of Borrower or such other party, whether now existing or hereafter arising, and Guarantor(s) agree that any such claim, defense, right of off-set shall be secondary and subordinate in right of payment to the prior payment in full of the Obligations.

This Agreement is a continuing guaranty and shall remain in full force and be binding upon Guarantor(s), notwithstanding the death of one or more thereof, until written notice of discontinuance shall have been received by Bank and until all Obligations existing or which Bank was committed to make before receipt of such notification shall have been paid in full as contemplated under this Agreement.

Guarantor(s) grant to Bank a security interest in all property of Guarantor(s) now or at any time hereafter in the possession of Bank to secure any liability of Guarantor(s) hereunder, and Bank shall have the rights and remedies of a secured party under The Uniform Commercial Code in respect to such property, including without limitation the right to sell or otherwise dispose of any or all of such property. Bank may apply or set off any deposit or other indebtedness at any time credited by or due from Bank to any of the Guarantor(s) against any liability of any of the Guarantor(s) under this Agreement. Such deposits or other indebtedness may at all times be held and treated as collateral security for the payment of any liability of any of the Guarantor(s) hereunder.

This Guaranty is further secured by a Deed of Trust and/or Security Agreement dated _____
made by Guarantors in favor of Bank and covering the following property: _____

This Agreement shall be construed as a continuing, absolute and unconditional guaranty of payment, without regard to the validity, regularity or enforceability of any of the Obligations, this Agreement or any other guaranty, surety, pledge, assignment or security for any of the Obligations, or any action taken or not taken by Bank and regardless of how long before or after the date hereof the Obligations were or are incurred. Bank, at its option, may proceed in the first instance against Guarantor(s) jointly and severally and have its remedy under this Agreement without being obligated to resort first to any security or any other remedy to enforce payment or collection of any of the Obligations, it being understood that Guarantor(s) jointly and severally are primarily liable for the payment when due of the Obligations. No delay in making demand on the Guarantor(s) for satisfaction of their liability hereunder shall prejudice Bank's right to enforce such satisfaction. All of Bank's rights and remedies shall be cumulative and any failure of the Bank to exercise any right hereunder shall not be construed as a waiver of the right to exercise the same or any other right at any time, and from time to time, thereafter.

The obligations of each of the Guarantor(s) under this Agreement and those of any other Guarantor(s) who may have guaranteed or who hereafter guarantee any of the Obligations are and will be joint and several, and Bank may release or settle with one or more of the Guarantor(s) at any time without affecting the existing liability of the remaining Guarantor(s).

Any notice or consent required or permitted by this Agreement shall be in writing and shall be deemed delivered if delivered in person or if sent by registered mail, postage pre-paid, return receipt requested, as follows, unless such address is changed by written notice hereunder:

(a) If to Bank:

                Attention:

(b) If to the Guarantor(s):

Guarantor(s) waive trial by jury with respect to any action, claim, suit or proceeding in respect of, or arising out of, this Agreement or any document executed in connection with, or relating to, the Obligation.

This Agreement shall be governed by, and construed in accordance with, the laws of the State of West Virginia.

This Agreement shall inure to the benefit of Bank, its successors and assigns, and to any person to whom Bank may grant an interest in the Obligations, and shall be binding upon the Guarantor(s) and their respective heirs, successors and assigns.

Special Provisions: _____
_____
_____
_____
_____.

IN WITNESS WHEREOF, the Guarantor(s), intending to be jointly and severally legally bound hereby, have duly executed this Agreement as of the _____ day of _____, 20_____.

BANK:

_____

By: _____

Its: _____

GUARANTOR(S):

_____

_____

_____

_____

Statement of Purpose for an Extension of Credit Secured By Margin Stock

---

Name of Bank

(Federal Reserve Form U-1)

This form is required by law (15 U.S.C. §§78g and 78w; 12 CFR 221).

INSTRUCTIONS

1. This form must be completed when a bank extends credit in excess of $100,000 secured directly or indirectly, in whole or in part, by any margin stock.

2. The term "margin stock" is defined in Regulation U (12 CFR 221) and includes, principally: (1) stocks that are registered on a national securities exchange or that are on the Federal Reserve Board's List of Marginable OTC Stocks; (2) debt securities (bonds) that are convertible into margin stocks; (3) any over-the-counter security designated as qualified for trading in the National Market System under a designation plan approved by the Securities and Exchange Commission (NMS security); and (4) shares of mutual funds, unless 95 per cent of the assets of the fund are continuously invested in U.S. government, agency, state, or municipal obligations.

3. Please print or type (if space is inadequate, attach separate sheet).

PART I. *To be completed by borrower(s).*

1. What is the amount of the credit being extended? _____

2. Will any part of this credit be used to purchase or carry margin stock? ☐ Yes ☐ No

If the answer is "no," describe the specific purpose of the credit. _____

_____

_____

_____

I (we) have read this form and certify that to the best of my (our) knowledge and belief the information given is true, accurate, and complete, and that the margin stock and any other securities collateralizing this credit are authentic, genuine, unaltered, and not stolen, forged, or counterfeit.

Signed: _____   Signed: _____

Borrower's Signature   Date   Borrower's Signature   Date

Print or Type Name   Print or Type Name

This form should not be signed in blank.

A borrower who falsely certifies the purpose of a credit on this form or otherwise willfully or intentionally evades the provisions of Regulation U will also violate Federal Reserve Regulation X, "Borrowers of Securities Credit."

1. List the margin stock securing this credit; do not include debt securities convertible into margin stock. The maximum loan value of margin stock is .... per cent of its current market value under the current Supplement to Regulation U.

No. of shares	Issue	Market price per share	Date and source of valuation (See note below)	Total market value per issue

2. List the debt securities convertible into margin stock securing this credit. The maximum loan value of such debt securities is .... per cent of the current market value under the current Supplement to Regulation U.

Principal amount	Issue	Market price	Date and source of valuation (See note below)	Total market value per issue

3. List other collateral including nonmargin stock securing this credit.

Describe briefly	Market price	Date and source of valuation (See note below)	Good faith loan value

Note: Bank need not complete "Date and source of valuation" if the market value was obtained from regularly published information in a journal of general circulation.

PART III. *To be signed by a bank officer in all instances.*

I am a duly authorized officer of the bank and understand that this credit secured by margin stock may be subject to the credit restrictions of Regulation U. I have read this form and any attachments, and I have accepted the customer's statement in Part I in good faith as required by Regulation U*, and I certify that to the best of my knowledge and belief, all the information given is true, accurate, and complete. I also certify that if any securities that directly secure the credit are not or will not be registered in the name of the borrower or its nominee, I have or will cause to have examined the written consent of the registered owner to pledge such securities. I further certify that any securities that have been or will be physically delivered to the bank in connection with this credit have been or will be examined, that all validation procedures required by bank policy and the Securities Exchange Act of 1934 (section 17(f), as amended) have been or will be performed, and that I am satisfied to the best of my knowledge and belief that such securities are genuine and not stolen or forged and their faces have not been altered.

Signed:

_____
Date

_____
Bank officer's signature

_____
Title

_____
Print or type name

*To accept the customer's statement in good faith, the officer of the bank must be alert to the circumstances surrounding the credit and, if in possession of any information that would cause a prudent person not to accept the statement without inquiry, must have investigated and be satisfied that the statement is truthful. Among the facts which would require such investigation are receipt of the statement through the mail or from a third party.

This form must be retained by the bank for at least three years after the credit is extinguished.

IRREVOCABLE STOCK OR BOND POWER

FOR VALUE RECEIVED, the undersigned does (do) hereby sell, assign and transfer to _____

_____

If stock, complete this portion	<_____ shares of the _____ <stock of _____ <_____ <Certificate(s) No. _____ <Standing in the name of the undersigned on the books of said company.

If bond, complete this portion	<Bond(s) of _____ <in the principal amount of $_____, <Serial No(s). _____ <Standing in the name of the undersigned on the books of said company.

      The undersigned does (do) hereby jointly and severally, irrevocably constitute and appoint _____, its successors or assigns, as the undersigned's attorney to transfer the said stock or bond, as the case may be, on the books of said company, with full power of substitution in the premises. The power is given to the holder hereof to fill in any and all blanks in this instrument. The Bank is authorized to make photocopies of this agreement as frequently and in such quantity as Bank shall deem appropriate. Each photocopy shall have the same force and effect as an original.

Signature guaranteed:

                                 _____(SEAL)
                                    Owner (as name appears on stock or bond)

_____

                                 _____(SEAL)
                                    Owner (as name appears on stock or bond)
                       Date:_____

CONSENT TO PLEDGE OR HYPOTHECATE

(Miscellaneous Collateral)

TO THE _____
_____(hereinafter "Bank")_____

_____, WEST VIRGINIA

_____, 20____

In order to induce you to extend credit to _____

_____

(hereinafter called the "Borrower"), I hereby unconditionally agree that the following property:

_____
_____
_____
_____

of which I am the owner, together with any proceeds thereof, dividends, interest or distribution relating thereto or earned thereon and any renewal, replacement or substitution may be pledged or hypothecated and delivered to you as collateral security for any and all obligations and liabilities of the Borrower to you, whether now existing or hereafter arising, direct or contingent, due or to become due, and any extension or renewal thereof, upon any terms and conditions whatsoever and with the same force and effect as if said property were owned by said Borrower. I further specifically agree that such property may be received, held and disposed of by you subject and pursuant to all terms and conditions of any and all notes, contracts, or agreements heretofore or hereafter signed by said Borrower as maker, endorser or guarantor or in any other capacity including all extensions and renewals thereof, and authorize and empower you from time to time to take any and all action with respect to such property authorized by the terms of any such agreement and without notice to me.

I hereby waive notice of the making, renewal or extending of any loan or financial accommodation to said Borrower. No forbearance shall act as a release of such collateral.

Without limiting your powers in dealing with said collateral, I authorize you to act solely upon the instructions of said Borrower relative to the sale or other disposition of said property, or any part thereof, or any substitutes therefore, or any proceeds thereof, and the receipt or acquittance of said Borrower for said property or any part thereof, or any substitute therefore, or any proceeds thereof, shall be valid and sufficient release and discharge of your liability.

Bank shall be deemed to have fulfilled its obligations with respect to the property pledged by me if it takes such action as I may request in writing, but no failure to such action shall, standing alone be a breach of Bank's obligation. No failure by Bank to take any action not requested in writing by me shall be a breach by the Bank of its obligation. Bank shall not be responsible for any decline in value of the collateral due to market conditions.

I further agree to deliver to you without demand therefore any additional certificates or shares, which I might receive by reason of my ownership of the above property whether by reason of a stock dividend, "stock split" or any other refinancing and such other or additional shares shall be held under the same terms and conditions herein set out.

_____   _____
Witness   Signature

193

Before you purchase a piece of property, you ask yourself many questions:

. Is it well located for my purposes?
. Is the purchase price right?
. What improvements will be necessary?

With the enactment of federal legislation that may hold you responsible for contamination of the property by prior owners, you will also want to know,

. Is there a possibility that hazardous wastes have ever been generated, stored, or disposed of on this piece of land or on adjacent properties?

SUPERFUND: ITS IMPACT ON LAND OWNERS

The 1980 Comprehensive Environmental Response, Compensation, and Liability Act (CERCLA, or Superfund) imposes strict liability on the owners of real property contaminated by hazardous materials--without regard to fault. The law imposes liability on other parties, particularly the prior owner who caused the contamination. However, if these parties cannot be located or are judgment-proof, the current owner may be held liable for all cleanup costs.

INNOCENT PURCHASER DEFENSE

In 1986, Congress adopted the Superfund Amendments and Reauthorization Act (SARA) to clarify some issues in the original Superfund legislation. SARA explicitly provides a defense to the liability of innocent purchasers for cleanup costs of contaminated property. The land owner must establish, however, that he or she did not know--nor had any reason to know--that the property was contaminated before it was acquired. The land owner must be able to demonstrate that, prior to acquiring the property, appropriate inquiry was made into the previous ownership and uses of the property, consistent with good commercial and customary practices.

INVESTIGATIONS

We suggest you contact environmental experts and your attorney to determine the nature and extent of the inquiry you should undertake for each property transfer transaction. Good commercial practice requires an inspection of the property for obvious signs of contamination: stressed vegetation; unusual coloration or odors in water; the presence of storage drums and tanks (above and under-ground); evidence of petroleum or oil products; and other signs would indicate the possiblity of contamination. You should also talk to the seller, the realtor, and other people with knowledge of the property. The questions on the reverse are suggested as a starting point for your inquiry. These, and other questions we may ask, represent a cursory investigation and are not a substitute for more formal, comprehensive environmental audits.

Possible sources of information about the property include the seller, the realtor, former owners or operators, owners/operators of adjoining sites, and local, state, and federal environmental protection agencies. Please consult your attorney and environmental experts for guidance in conducting a due diligence inquiry and in determining your potential liability for any environmental cleanup.

1) Is this property a registered or proposed Superfund (CERCLA) site?

2) Has this property been identified by a state or local environmental agency as a site requiring enviromental investigation or cleanup?

3) Has this property been the subject of any environmental regulatory enforcement action?

4) Has this property been used for any industrial, manufacturing or agricultural purpose or as a landfill?

5) Have any past owners of this property generated, stored, or disposed of hazardous substances or regulated materials on this property?

6) Are any neighboring properties used for any business involved in the generation, storage or disposal of hazardous substances or regulated materials?

7) In addition to its past uses, do you plan to use this property for any business involved in the generation, storage or disposal of hazardous substances or regulated materials? If yes, do you have procedures that meet regulatory requirements for proper handling of these materials?

_____   _____
Account Officer Signature   Borrower Signature (if applicable)

ENVIRONMENTAL CERTIFICATIONS

Borrower certifies by acceptance of this agreement, or will furnish evidence satisfactory to Bank, that the property does not contain (a) asbestos in any form, (b) urea formaldehyde foam insulation, (c) transformers or other equipment containing polychlorinated biphenyls (PCBs) in amounts that exceed acceptable standard levels, (d) underground storage tanks, (e) nor any other materials or substances that are regulated or prohibited by Federal, State, or local laws, or that are known to pose a hazard to the environment or to human health.

Borrower also certifies, or will furnish evidence satisfactory to Bank, that the property and operations at the property are in compliance with all applicable Federal, State, and local statutes, laws, and regulations. Borrower further certifies that no notices claiming a violation of regulations or statutes, nor notices requiring compliance with regulations or statutes, nor notices demanding payment or contribution for injury to the environment or human health have been served on Borrower, or to the best of Borrower's knowledge, on any former owner/operator of the property, by any government agency, individual, or other entity. Borrower agrees to forward a copy of any such notices received after settlement to Bank within three (3) days of their receipt. Borrower acknowledges that Bank shall not be obligated to make any disbursements if condemnation proceedings are commenced or threatened against any part of the property.

Borrower further certifies that any hazardous or potentially hazardous materials used in Borrower's operation or generated as a product or by-product are now and will continue to be stored, used, and maintained in accordance with applicable Federal, State, and local laws and regulations and that all hazardous wastes will be disposed of by duly licensed contractors in accordance with all governing regulations. In the sole and absolute discretion of Bank, Borrower may be required to submit a report, satisfactory to Bank, prepared by a consultant acceptable to Bank, certifying that Borrower has complied and is complying with this clause. Bank further reserves the right to require systematic and periodic monitoring of the property throughout the term of the loan.

By execution of the Deed of Trust at loan closing, Borrower shall provide additional warranties and representations concerning the environmental conditons of the Property. Borrower shall also indemnify Bank against any and all damages arising from any claims of environmental contamination of the property.

Agreed and accepted this the _____ day of _____, 20_____.

_____

By: _____

Its:_____

_____
_____
_____

NOTICE OF ASSIGNMENT OF
ACCOUNTS RECEIVABLES

NOTICE is hereby given that _____ (hereinafter "Borrower") has granted _____ (hereinafter "Bank") a security interest in and assignment of all right, title and interest of Borrower in all accounts receivable, contract rights, chattel paper and other payments due or to become due from you _____ payable to Borrower whether now existing or hereafter arising.

By agreement of _____, as evidenced by Borrower's acknowledgement below, you are hereby authorized, instructed and directed to remit all payments and future payments due and payable to Borrower in their entirety to _____ at the following address:

_____
_____
_____
_____

This agreement has no expiration and is not deemed canceled unless expressly canceled in writing by Bank.

Acknowledged and received this _____ day of _____, 20____.

_____(Bank)

By: _____

Its: _____

_____(Borrower)

By: _____

Its: _____

By: _____

Its: _____

BORROWING BASE CERTIFICATE

1. Beginning Balance, Total Receivables outstanding $ _____
   Assigned to Lender (use Previous Report Line 4)
2. Additions to Accounts Receivable
   A. New Billings   _____
   B. Credit Memos   _____
   C. Other   _____   _____
3. Deductions from Accounts Receivable.
   A. Net Invoices Paid (Collection No. _____)   _____
   B. Other   _____ $ _____
4. Total Receivables Outstanding Assigned to LENDER
5. Assigned Collateral Adjustments.
   A. Delinquents   _____
   B. Other Ineligible Accounts   _____ $ _____
6. Total Accounts Receivable Eligible for Loan
7. Other Assets Eligible for Loan.
   A. Inventories   _____
   B. Other   _____
8. TOTAL COLLATERAL ELIGIBLE FOR LOAN (Line 6 + 7) $ _____
   ==========

- -

LOAN STATUS

9. Available Loan Advance.
   A. Accounts Receivable @ ____% of Line 6   _____
   B. Inventories @ _____% of Line 7A.   _____
   C. Other Assets @ _____% of Line 7B. $ _____

10. TOTAL LOAN BALANCE $ _____

11. Additional Loan Requested   _____

12. TOTAL NEW LOAN BALANCE: $ _____
13. Credit Line $ _____

14. BALANCE AVAILABLE FOR LOAN (Line 9 or line 14 - $ _____
    whichever is less-minus line 13.)

For the purpose of inducing _____ (hereinafter Bank) as the
case may be to grant loans to us pursuant to the terms of our Agreement dated _____, we
hereby certify that the foregoing statement of our accounts described above is true and correct and according to the books and
records of the company and is available as acceptable collateral for loans in accordance with the representations and warranties
set forth in Agreement. The Loan Balance shown on Line 13 above accurately reflects our indebtedness for advances under the
above Agreement subject to charges by the BANK.

CLIENT _____

Date _____

By:_____
            Authorized Signature

Delivered to and accepted by BANK at _____, WV
     This _____ day of _____, 20____.

BY _____

Glossary

Accounts payable money owed by you to your suppliers.

Accounts receivable money owed to you by customers.

Accruals items that are due but unpaid of the date of a financial statement.

Automated Clearing House an electronic payment and collection network.

Available balance that portion of the balance in your account that remains after the collected balance has been reduced by the Federal Reserve Bank's reserve requirement.

Capital ratio total shareholder equity as a percent of total assets.

Charge-off a rate of loss on outstanding loans that banks consider acceptable and provide for in their budgets; today, charge-off ratios of one-half percent are common.

Clean-up paying off all borrowings under a line of credit for a specified period of time.

Collateral security put up by a borrower that can compensate a bank if the borrower defaults on the loan.

Collected balances balances on which funds have already been transferred from the issuing bank to the receiving bank.

Common ratios ratios that relate balance-sheet and profit and loss items to one common figure.

Compensating balance an amount required to be left in an account so that the bank can invest and earn income on it to use to offset operating expenses.

Country risk the possibility that a country in which you have business dealings may experience political or economic instability.

Credit risk the possibility that a borrower may not be able to repay a loan.

Current ratio current assets divided by current liabilities. Two to one is the classic value for the current ratio.

Debt ratios ratios that relate indebtedness to capital.

Deferred funds funds that have been deposited to your account but that may not be withdrawn for a certain period of time; common requirement for new accounts.

Delta ratios ratios that show changes from one date to another in items such as total assets, total liabilities, net worth, gross or net sales, and net income.

Demand loan a loan on which a bank can demand full payment at any time.

Depository transfer check a check drawn on an outlying bank that moves funds from it to a central bank account.

Direct deposit account an account into which deposits are made by someone other than the owner of the account.

Draft a written order by the buyer, your customer, telling an overseas bank to pay you upon release of certain required documents. May be a *sight* draft or a *time* draft.

Financial statements financial reports prepared by companies; comprise the balance sheet and the income and expense statement (also called the profit and loss statement).

Foreign currency exchange risk the possibility that payment you receive in foreign currency will decline in value from the time you sign a contract to the time you actually receive payment because of normal fluctuations in currency values.

Goodwill the excess of what you paid for an asset over its book value.

Guardianship trust a trust created to provide complete financial management for someone who is considered legally incompetent.

HR-10 accounts the account part of HR-10 retirement plans; also known as Keogh accounts.

Ledger balances balances that are included in the overall balance figure on your statement even though they have not yet been collected by your bank from the issuing bank.

Letter of credit a letter outlining the terms of an extension of credit, usually from your customer's bank to you.

Life insurance trust a trust that provides funds to your estate to avoid an unwanted liquidation of assets solely in order to meet obligations, such as taxes.

Liquidity the ease with which an investment can be converted to cash.

Living trust a legal entity you create to own property and use it for the benefit of someone else.

Loan guarantee a legally binding agreement by an outside source to make good on a loan if the borrower defaults.

Loan-to-deposit ratio the dollar amount of a bank's outstanding loans as a percentage of the total dollars on deposit; an important measure of a bank's loan activity.

Lock box a rented box from which your bank retrieves payments to you several times during the day and deposits them to your account, guaranteeing you maximum return on those funds because their deposit is accelerated.

Net interest income the single largest source of income for a bank; includes interest on loans and investments owned by the bank less interest incurred on deposits, certificates of deposit, and money borrowed outright.

Open account an arrangement in which you ship goods without receiving payment or a written promise to pay and without retaining title to the goods.

Qualified terminable interest trust (QTIP) a trust that can shelter assets that do not qualify for the marital deduction on a spouse's estate.

Quick ratio current assets less current inventory divided by current liabilities. One to one is considered optimal.

Rate risk the possibility that interest rates will fluctuate; variable rates protect the bank from rate risk.

Return on assets ratio the bank's net income for the year as percentage of its total assets.

Return on equity ratio the bank's net income as a percentage of the bank's total capital, including common stock, preferred stock, and retained earnings.

Spread the difference between what the bank pays for its deposits and what it earns on its loans and deposits.

Subordinated debt debt that has subordinated some of its rights to those of other creditors.

Sweep account an account in which the balance at the end of the day is invested overnight in an investment which is undone in the morning, freeing your funds.

Testamentary trust one created in a will that does not take effect until the maker of the will dies.

Turnover ratios ratios that measure the speed with which you pay your suppliers and your customers pay you as well as the relationship between inventory and sales.

Uncollected item a financial instrument that has been deposited at one bank but which the issuing bank has not yet paid, thereby completing the transfer of funds.

Zero balance accounts accounts that maintain no balance until checks are presented to the account for payment, at which time the necessary funds are transferred to it.

INTERNET RESOURCES
Federal Agencies

Federal Deposit Insurance Corporation
www.fdic.gov

Federal Reserve Board of Governors
www.bog.frb.fed.us

Office of the Comptroller of the Currency
www.occ.treas.gov

Small Business Administration
www.sba.gov

Industry Financial Ratios
Dun & Bradstreet, Inc.
www.dnb.com

Robert Morris Associates
www.rmahq.org

Credit Ratings
Fitch IBCA
www.fitchibca.com

Moody's Investor Service
www.moodys.com

Standard & Poor's
www.standardandpoors.com

International Trade
International Chamber of Commerce
www.iccwbo.org

Bank Rating Organizations
Bauer Group
www.bauerfinancial.com

IDC Financial Publishing
www.idcfp.com

LACE Financial Corp.
www.lacefincl.com

Sheshunoff Information Services
www.sheshunoff.com

SNL Securities
www.snl.com

Thomson Financial Bankwatch
www.bankwatch.com

Veribanc
www.veribanc.com

Selected Further Reading

Dawson, George M., *Borrowing to Build Your Business, Getting Your Banker to Say "Yes,"* Upstart Publishing Co., 1997.

Evanson, David R., *Where to Go When the Bank Says No, Alternatives for Financing Your Business,* Bloomberg Press, 1998.

Flanagan, Lawrence, *The Money Connection, Where and How to Apply for Business Loans and Venture Capital,* The Oasis Press, 1995.

Goldsick, Gary, *Romancing the Business Loan, Getting Your Banker to Say "Yes" in the 1990s,* Lexington Books, 1994.

Lacey, Harold R., *Other People's Money, How and Where to Find Money for Start-Up and Growing Businesses,* Sage Creek Press, 1998.

O'Hara, Patrick D., *SBA Loans, A Step-by-Step Guide,* Third Edition, John Wiley & Sons, Inc., 1998.

Smith, Andrew M., and Dennis M. Suchocki, *Banking Smarter: How to Save Money in Your Banking Relationship,* BCS and Associates, 1994.

Index

About the Authors

Theodore A. Platz, Jr., a graduate of Dartmouth College and the Graduate School of Business Administration at New York University, has been a commercial lender for much of his career. He began at Chase Manhattan Bank in 1955 and worked as a loan officer in its Aviation Department and its National Division before moving to Franklin National Bank in 1964 and participating in its aggressive financing of small businesses on Long Island. In 1977, he joined Charleston National Bank, one of the largest commercial lenders in West Virginia, and later became its president. He is the former Vice Chairman of Key Centurion Bancshares, Inc., the largest bank holding company in West Virginia.

Thomas P. Fitch has written and contributed to numerous articles and books on banking and finance. He is the author of *Barron's Dictionary of Banking Terms.* A graduate of Fairfield University, he lives in Connecticut.